# Sew the Storybook Wardrobe
## for 18-Inch Dolls

## Joan Hinds & Jean Becker

**Krause Publications**
700 East State St., Iola, WI 54990-0001
Telephone (715) 445-2214
www.krause.com

Please call or write for our free catalog of publications. Our toll-free number to place an order or obtain a free catalog is 800-258-0929 or please use our regular business telephone 715-445-2214 for editorial comment and further information.

Printed in the United States of America

Library of Congress Catalog Number: 99-61445

ISBN: 0-87341-730-5

The following registered trademark terms and companies appear in this publication:

*American Girl*™ *by Pleasant Company, Apple Valley Friends*™ *by Apple Valley Doll Works, Barbie®, Chatty Cathy®, Creative Doll Company®, Engelpuppen®, Faithful Friends*™ *by Heidi Ott, Götz®, Kleenex®, RickRack®, Shirley Temple®, Storybook Heirlooms*™*, Toni®, Ultrasuede®, Velcro®.*

# Acknowledgments

Once again, a heartfelt thank you to Kathy Marsaa, our illustrator, for making sense out of nonsense; to Steve Tiggemann from Jeff Frey & Associates Photography of Duluth, Minnesota, for helping us set the stage; to our parents, Don and Nina Sudor, and Carl and Selma Nylund, who urged (ordered?) us to use our imaginations; and to our husbands and children for their patience and unlimited support.

# Introduction

Somewhere along the way, we both were encouraged to use our imaginations. Probably our parents had a lot to do with that. ("Can't you kids go outside and find *something to **do***?!") We didn't have electronic toys, computerized games, and videos to keep us busy. We also didn't have nonstop, double-booked activity schedules and limitless cash. ("A second car? Do you think money grows on *trees*?!") And if that special toy we saw advertised on TV wasn't stocked in the toy department of the local hardware store, well, we'd just have to get along without it. Probably the city kids could get it, but we couldn't. Barbie and all our other dolls would have to make do with homemade outfits.

So began our ultimately merging careers in doll costume design. Even before either one of us could sew, Toni wore a shawl that was really a person's wool scarf when she pretended to be a pioneer girl. When Chatty Cathy wanted to be a Beatle groupie, she had a miniskirt that was cut from an oversize neon green sock. Shirley Temple had a crown made from construction paper when she portrayed a princess. And Barbie, well, she wore a lot of creative pastel designs made from Kleenex. Lucky thing she was so small. Hem? What's a hem?

And then, of course, we both did an enormous amount of reading. Storybooks open the world - past, present, and future. Once you have all those stories rattling around in your head, you just have to act them out. Even if your human playmates aren't available, a cast of dolls can play all the parts.

Now that we've learned to sew, we'd like to share some of our dramatic costumes and play setting ideas with you. But this book is just the beginning. Let your own imagination take you to storybooks other than the ones portrayed here and add more characters. So turn off that TV, fire up the sewing machine, and enter the world of make believe. (Let the kids play too.)

*Joan Hinds    Jean Becker*

## Measuring 18-Inch Dolls

*Even within a single brand, measurements may vary from doll to doll when dealing with a stuffed cloth body because the bodies don't come from a mold and there is a human element involved in their fullness. In most instances, the most critical measurement (other than height, which you can easily adjust for by reducing or increasing hems) is the waist. This becomes most important when making pants and skirts with waistbands - dresses tend to be loose enough to accommodate variations.*

*For instance, a random selection of eight Pleasant Company dolls revealed waist measurements of 10⅝", 11", 11⅛", 11¼", 11⅜", 11½", another 11½", and even 12"! We've noticed that older dolls seem to be slimmer than newer ones, although some of the difference may be due to compression of the stuffing from being played with or from doll stands gripping them tightly. Other brands yielded variations in the same range. The Magic Attic Club dolls have a 9¼" waistline, which is out of the ball park completely and cannot use these patterns without alteration.*

# Table of Contents

# Before You Begin

I t is now 13 years since the first American Girl doll was released by Pleasant Company, triggering a phenomenal rebirth of childlike play dolls. Of course, dolls had never really gone away, but the market had been dominated for years by 11½" fashion dolls, such as Barbie, with decidedly adult bodies.

Today there are many manufacturers of the type known as "18-inch modern vinyl playable child dolls." Their faces are all unique, but the basic cloth bodies are sufficiently similar to be able to exchange clothing, particularly dresses. Arms, legs, hands, and feet sometimes vary enough to require different sleeve lengths and different shoe sizes, but most of them can wear the costumes in this book.

As long as this type of doll remains popular, more brands will appear each year. Be aware that they might require slight adjustments in waistbands, hem lengths, and elastic measurements for sleeves. The patterns in this book presume a 11½" waist. Try things on your doll as you construct the garments to make sure of the fit and accommodate variances.

Remember that although human garments usually have ⅝" seam allowances, doll garment seam allowances are ¼" unless specifically indicated otherwise. We have found that the so-called ¼" seam allowances produced by most people are actually closer to ⅜", and this can cause problems when multiplied by all the seams. To guarantee a perfect ¼" seam allowance, we recommend using a quilting foot.

When sewing parts of a garment together, you usually pin them right sides together, but there are exceptions, so read carefully.

Select your fabric carefully and prewash it if you are using 100% cotton. Most doll clothes that are to be played with will need laundering eventually and you don't want them to shrink.

When our instructions say "press" or "clip the curves and trim the seams," please don't skip these seemingly insignificant instructions. They make a big difference in the final appearance of your project.

Whenever we tell you to use a serger to sew a seam or finish a fabric edge, you can use a simple zigzag or machine stitch appropriate for knit garments. When sewing on very stretchable fabrics, you definitely must choose an elastic stitch or serge.

In many garments, we recommend a lined bodice. This means cutting out twice as many front and back pieces, but it's much easier than applying facings in a small garment.

Never sew the underarm seam of a doll dress and then try to set it into a bodice armhole. Always sew the sleeves to the armhole first, then sew the underarm seam, starting at the wrist or elbow and ending up at the bodice waistline.

If you are sewing costumes for a doll owned by a very young child, please don't attach anything to the costume that would be a choking hazard if it came off.

# Cinderella

# Cinderella's Kitchen Setting

Today's quilt shops have so many varieties of fabric that you can find a print to suit almost every need. We were astonished to find red brick, terra cotta brick, even yellow brick prints. And for the fireplace, we found a stonework print (which also worked out well for the castle in Alice in Wonderland).

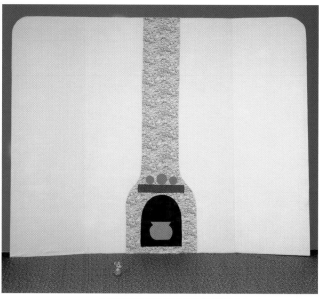

## Supplies:

Cardboard project display board, 48" x 36"
1 1/3 yd. cream felt for walls
*Optional: 1 1/2 yd. brick print fabric for foreground*
Stonework print fabric for fireplace, 36" x 12"
Scraps of black and gray felt for fireplace and pot
Scraps of fabric for fireplace shelf and plates
Gray polymer clay for mouse
2 blue rhinestones or glass-headed pins for mouse's eyes
Spray adhesive
Craft glue stick

## Setting

Pattern pieces 1, 2, 3

**1.** Following the manufacturer's instructions, spray adhesive sparingly over the entire front of the display board. Let it dry a bit before you stretch the felt over the board, working out any bubbles with your fingers. Trim away excess felt along the cardboard edges.
**2.** Cut out a fireplace and use spray adhesive to apply it to the background. Cut out the

firebox shape from black felt and the pot from gray felt. Glue stick them in place. Add a shelf and three plates cut from other fabric scraps. Glue them in place.

## Mouse

*(soon to become a coachman)*

**1.** Following the manufacturer's instructions, mold a mouse body, head, ears, and tail from gray polymer clay. Insert rhinestone or glass-head pins for eyes, then bake as directed. To keep it simple (and not reveal our total lack of sculpting skills), this mouse has no limbs, but he sits up nicely anyway.

# Cinderella's Enchanted Evening Setting

As soon as you can summon the Fairy Godmother and her wand, turn that mouse into a coachman and get Cinderella ready for the ball! If you have a doll willing to play the part of the Prince, you could make a small satin pillow for the glass slipper. Read the story again and add whatever other characters and props you can make or find around the house.

# Supplies:

Cardboard project display board, 48" x 36"

1½ yd. midnight blue taffeta with gold stars

*Optional:* 1½ yd. grass print fabric for foreground

Scraps of dark green printed fabric for distant hills

Scrap of stonework print fabric for path

⅓ yd. white iridescent satin for coach

Scraps of gold lamé fabric with knit backing for wheels, door, and windows of coach

Scraps of fabric for moon and clouds

½ yd. gold lace (1¼"-wide)

⅓ yd. gold trim (⅝"-wide)

Scraps of orange and green fabrics for pumpkins

Gray polymer clay for mouse

2 blue rhinestones or glass-headed pins for mouse's eyes

Spray adhesive

Craft glue stick

# Setting

Pattern pieces  4, 5, 6, 7, 8, 9, 10, 11, 12, 13, 14

**1.** Cut your "starry night" fabric so it fits the display board plus about 2" around all edges. Following the manufacturer's instructions, spray adhesive sparingly over the entire front of the display board. Let it dry a bit before you attempt to lay the fabric out on it because if it is too wet, it can spot the fabric. Stretch the fabric out over the board, working out any bubbles with your fingers. You can usually lift the fabric up and reposition it if necessary.

Use a glue stick to secure the raw edges of the fabric to the back side of the board.

**2.** Cut out distant hills from green fabric and glue in place on the front as you please.

**3.** Because the fabric is so thin, you'll need to cut out two coaches from the white iridescent satin and glue stick them together. Then glue them to the background with spray adhesive.

**4.** Glue the narrower gold trim to the background over the lower edge of the coach and curving up on each end to create wheel wells. Cut out wheels from the gold lamé and glue them in place.

**5.** Cut a piece of gold lace to fit across the roof of the coach and glue it in place. Glue a shorter piece at the top of the coach so it looks like a crown.

**6.** Cut out a door and two windows from gold lamé and glue them in place.

**7.** Cut out a moon and clouds and glue them where you like.

**8.** Cut out pumpkins from various orange fabrics (adding texture with crinkly organdy overlays is fun) and glue them to the background.

**9.** Cut a path from the stonework print fabric and lay it out in the foreground as desired.

# Mouse

**1.** Following the manufacturer's instructions, mold a mouse body, head, ears, and tail from gray polymer clay. Insert rhinestone or glass-head pins for eyes, then bake as directed.

# Poor Cinderella

Our poor Cinderella is color-coordinated, but you could use fabric leftovers of any kind. Check out the remnant basket for bits and pieces of "peasant" materials.

*The model is a Engelpuppen doll.*

# Supplies:

**Blouse**
1/4 yd. cream broadcloth
9" elastic (1/8"-wide)
3 snaps or Velcro

**Skirt**
1/3 yd. calico
1 hook and eye or Velcro

**Vest**
1/4 yd. broadcloth
20" ribbon (1/8"-wide)
3 snaps or Velcro

**Apron and Scarf**
1/2 yd. broadcloth

**Broom**
8" dowel, 3/8"-diameter for broomstick
Children's watercolor paints and brush
Raffia scraps

# Blouse

Pattern pieces 15, 16, 17

**1.** Cut one front, two backs, and two sleeves from the cream broadcloth. Right sides together, sew the front to the backs at the shoulder seams.
**2.** Press center back edges under 1/8". Press under another 1/8" and stitch.
**3.** Cut a matching bias strip 1" x 8¾". Pin it to the wrong side of the blouse neckline so that one long edge is flush with the neckline and the short ends extend 1/4" beyond the hemmed center backs. Stitch in place.
**4.** Grade the seam allowances. Tucking in the short ends, fold the bias over twice so it ends up on the right side of the blouse. Topstitch.

**5.** Zigzag or serge the bottom edge of each sleeve. Turn under and straight stitch (or use your rolled hem attachment) to hem the sleeves.
**6.** Cut the elastic in two 4½" lengths. Using a pencil, draw a line on the wrong side of the sleeve 3/4" above and parallel to the hemmed sleeve bottom. Using two or three straight stitches, anchor one end of the elastic to the fabric on the line. Switch to a wide enough zigzag stitch to swing back and forth over the elastic, creating a mini-casing. Stretch the elastic as you proceed to the end of the line; straight stitch the elastic to the fabric to anchor it at the end.

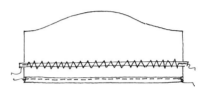

**7.** Gather the sleeve caps between *s. Right sides together, stitch the sleeves to the blouse armholes.

**8.** Right sides together, sew the underarm seams from the sleeve to the bottom edge of the blouse.

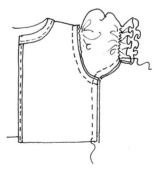

**9.** Hem the blouse by turning the bottom edge under 1/4" twice and stitching. Sew snaps or Velcro to the center backs, lapping right over left about 1/4".

# Skirt

**1.** Cut a 7½" x 30" rectangle from the skirt fabric. Cut a 1½" x 12½" waistband on grain.

**2.** Press one long edge of the skirt under ¼". Press under another ¼" and stitch.

**3.** Right sides together, sew the center back seam to within 3" of the unhemmed edge (the waist edge). Press the seam allowances open. Topstitch around the opening to finish it off.

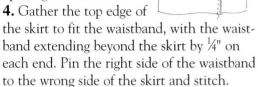

**4.** Gather the top edge of the skirt to fit the waistband, with the waistband extending beyond the skirt by ¼" on each end. Pin the right side of the waistband to the wrong side of the skirt and stitch.

**5.** Press the remaining long edge of the waistband under ¼". Fold it over so it ends up on the right side of the skirt, tucking in the short ends. Topstitch from the right side of the skirt.

**6.** Lapping the right center back over the left by about ¼" (or however much you need to for your particular doll), sew the hook and eye or Velcro to the waistband.

# Vest

Pattern pieces 18, 19

**1.** This lined vest laces up the front, but it also has a back opening so kids don't have to unlace the vest to change clothes. Cut out four backs and four fronts from the vest broadcloth.

**2.** Right sides together, stitch each back to a front at the shoulder seams so you have a vest and a lining in four parts. Press.

**3.** Right sides together, pin left and right vest parts to the left and right lining parts and stitch up the center fronts, around the neckline, and down the center backs. Then sew the armholes.

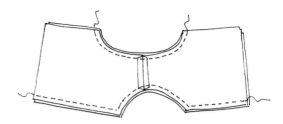

**4.** Stitch the side seams together by opening up the vest and lining at the side seams. Turn to the right side and press.

**5.** Press the bottom edges of both vests and linings ¼" toward the inside. Stitch the opening closed.

**6.** With a large-eyed needle, thread the ribbon and lace the vest fronts together, following the dots on the pattern piece. Tie the ends together at the bottom edge.

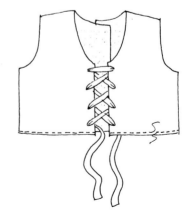

**7.** Sew snaps or Velcro to the center backs of the vest, lapping the right over the left approximately ¼".

## Apron

**1.** Cut a 5½" x 10" rectangle from the broadcloth. Cut a 1½" x 4½" waistband on grain. Cut two 1¼" x 18" ties on grain.

**2.** Hem one long edge and both short ends of the rectangle by pressing it under ¼" and topstitching. Gather the remaining long edge to fit the waistband, with the waistband extending beyond the gathered apron ¼" on each end.

**3.** Pin the right side of the waistband to the wrong side of the apron. Press the remaining long edge of the waistband under ¼". Set aside.

**4.** Narrow hem the long edges of each tie, either with your rolled hem attachment or by pressing it under ⅛" twice and stitching. Fold one end of each tie towards the wrong side at a 45° angle. Stitch. Cut off the excess fabric.

**5.** On the remaining short ends of the ties, make a pleat and pin it ½" inside where the waistband seam will be. Tuck in the short ends of the waistband ¼" on each end and enclose the pleated ends of the ties by folding the waistband over to the right side of the apron. Topstitch all three sides of the waistband.

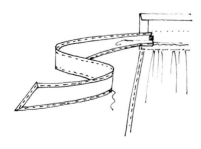

## Scarf

**1.** Cut a triangle 16½" on the long side and 11" on the remaining two sides.

**2.** Press the long edge under ¼" and stitch. Use pinking shears if you have them to cut along the remaining sides. Otherwise hem them like the first edge.

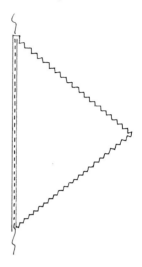

## Patches

**1.** Cut six ¾" squares with pinking shears if you have them. No need to hem them if you do not have pinkers. Use a glue stick or machine stitching and apply the patches at random to the vest and apron.

## Cinderella's Broom

**1.** Use children's watercolor paint to stain the 8" dowel brown. Rubber band a small handful of raffia to the bottom and wrap the rubber band with more raffia.

# Enchanted Cinderella

Designing a glass slipper is harder than you'd think. This one requires some skill with a glue gun, so it's not a project for young children. Another option would be to sew the slippers out of translucent organza. In that case, follow the instructions for Dorothy's Ruby Slippers on page 67.

*The model is a Götz doll.*

# Supplies:

2/3 yd. star print organza
2/3 yd. white taffeta
1/4 yd. gold trim (1/2"-wide)
1/2 yd. elastic (1/8"-wide)
3 2/3 yd. gold/silver trim (5/8"-wide)
Scrap of poster board for slippers
1/4 yd. medium weight clear vinyl purchased
    from the fabric store (make sure you can
    bend and curve it easily - too thin is better
    than too thick)
Gold craft paint
2 very small gold roses
3/4 yd. clear iridescent beads-by-the-yard
Hot glue gun

# Dress

Pattern pieces  20,  21,  22,  23,  24,  25

**1.** Cut out one front bodice and two back bodices from the organza. Cut out two front bodices and four back bodices from the taffeta.

**2.** Cut out one front overlay and one 10½" x 45" skirt from taffeta. Cut two sleeves, two peplums, and one 10½" x 45" overskirt from organza.

**3.** Layer the organza bodice pieces over one set of the taffeta ones, right sides up, and baste around all edges. You will treat this double layer as the bodice.

**4.** Right sides (organza layer to organza layer) together, sew the double-layered front bodice to the double-layered back bodices at the shoulder seams. Sew the remaining taffeta lining together at the shoulder seams also.

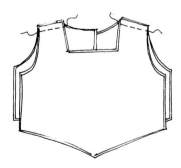

**5.** Pin the lining to the double-layered bodice, right sides together, and stitch up one center back, around the square neckline and down the other center back. Clip corners, trim seams, turn right side out, and press lightly with a cool iron.

**6.** Zigzag some 5/8"-wide trim across the top of the front overlay. Approximately 1" down from the top trim, zigzag some 1/2"-wide trim in a parallel line. Repeat twice more at 1" intervals.

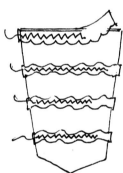

**7.** Baste the front overlay to the center front of the bodice along both sides. Pin 5/8"-wide trim over the sides of the front overlay and run it over the shoulder to the center back of the bodice. Zigzag in place.

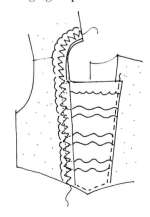

**8.** Pin ⅝"-wide lace to the lower edge of each sleeve, about ¼" up from the sleeve bottom. Zigzag in place.

**9.** Cut a 4½" piece of elastic and zigzag it directly to the wrong side of the sleeve, in a line 4" from the trimmed sleeve bottom. Cut a 4" piece of elastic and zigzag it in a line 2" above the trimmed sleeve bottom. Repeat with the other sleeve.

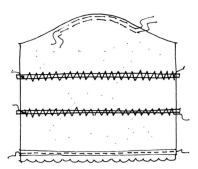

**10.** Gather the sleeve caps between *s and sew them to the bodice armholes, right sides together. Sew the underarm seams.

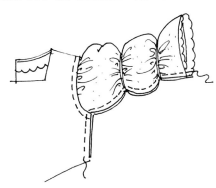

**11.** Narrow hem the taffeta skirt along one long edge.

**12.** With right sides up, pin the ⅝"-wide trim along one long edge of the organza overskirt so the lace overlaps the fabric by about ¼". Zigzag over the heading of the lace.

**13.** Layer the organza skirt over the taffeta one and treat them as one unit from now on. Right sides together, sew the center back seam of the skirt up to within 3" of the top edge. Press the seam allowances open and topstitch around the opening.

**14.** Press the curved edges of each peplum under ¼". Zigzag the ⅝"-wide lace to the curved edge as you did with the bottom of the organza overskirt.

**15.** Fold the layered skirt in half crosswise to locate the center front. Pin each peplum to the right side of the folded skirt with the trimmed curved edges just meeting in the center front. Using the basque waist guide (pattern piece #25), cut out a triangle to accommodate the point at the center front of the bodice, going through all the skirt and peplum layers. Then unpin the peplums from the skirt.

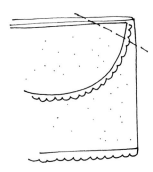

**16.** Gather the top of the skirt and the top edge of each peplum. Pull the gathering threads of the skirt so it fits the bodice. Pull the gathering threads of the peplums and pin them, right sides up, to the skirt. The curved edges of the peplums should meet in the center front of the skirt where the basque waist point cutout is. The center back edges of the peplums should stop ¾" from the center back opening of the skirt. Baste the gathered skirt and gathered peplums together. Right sides together, sew the completed skirt to the bodice.

**17.** Lapping the right over the left, sew three snaps to the back of the bodice.

# Glass Slippers

Pattern pieces 26, 27

**1.** Cut out four soles from poster board. Paint one side of each sole with gold paint. Remember to paint the cut edges of the poster board and make two lefts and two rights.

**2.** Cut two glass slipper uppers from the clear vinyl. Sew the heel seam in each. Turn right side out.

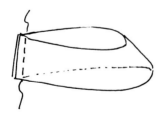

**3.** Slide the uppers on the doll's feet. Make ¼" slashes all around the bottom edge as shown.

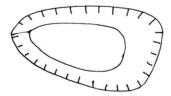

Put one set of soles against the doll's feet, gold side toward the doll. Dab hot glue around half a sole and fold the slashed upper so it is imbedded in the hot glue. Be careful not to burn yourself! Continue around the rest of the shoe, going back over the folded-in portion until the glue is completely hard. Repeat for the other shoe.

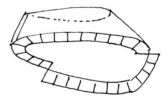

**4.** Hot glue the other set of soles to the outside of the shoes, gold side down. Be sure to press the soles together as tightly as you can so as to leave little space between them.

**5.** Run a bead of hot glue around the soles and decorate with beads or pearls-by-the-yard. Do the same around the top of each shoe, but reinforce that row of beads by whip-stitching them with gold or clear thread. Hot glue a gold rose to the front of each shoe.

# Fairy Godmother

With all the different shades of netting available in fabric stores, there's no end to the magical variations you can create.

*The model is a Götz doll.*

## Supplies:

½ yd. satin

1¼ yd. of netting (62"-wide) (netting with glitter and sparkle is best)

1 yd. silver trim (³/₈"-wide)

15" silver trim (½"-wide)

⅔ yd. each satin ribbon in two colors (¼"-wide)

7 small fabric roses

1 pipe cleaner for headband

3 snaps

Silver sequin-like fabric, 5" x 5"

Heavy interfacing, 5" x 5"

12" sequins-by-the-yard trim for wand

10" dowel, ¹/₁₆"-diameter for wand

Silver glitter paint

Hot glue gun

Fabric glue stick

## Dress

Pattern pieces 28, 29

**1.** Cut out two front bodices and four back bodices from the satin. This sleeveless dress is self-lined to eliminate facings.

**2.** Right sides together, sew one front bodice to two back bodices at the shoulder seams. Repeat for lining and set the lining aside.

**3.** Cut a 2" x 36" strip of the netting for the neck ruffle. Zigzag a 36" piece of the ³/₈"-wide trim to one long edge of the netting ruffle.

**4.** Gather the remaining long edge of the ruffle to fit the right side of the bodice neckline. Baste the ruffle in place.

**5.** Right sides together, pin the bodice lining to the bodice, with the ruffle in between. Making sure the ruffle is pinned out of the way so as not to catch it in the stitching, sew the lining to the bodice by stitching up one center back, around the neckline, and down the other center back.

**6.** Sew the bodice to its lining by stitching around the armholes. Clip curves and turn right side out.

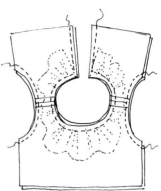

**7.** Right sides together, sew the bodice side seams, opening out the lining from the bodice.

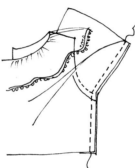

**8.** Cut a 9" x 45" rectangle of satin for the skirt. Narrow hem one long edge.

**9.** Right sides together, sew the center back seam of the skirt up to within 3" of the top. Press the seam allowances open. Topstitch around the opening.

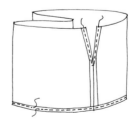

**10.** Cut four 10" x 56" rectangles of netting for the overskirt. Layering them and treating them as one piece of fabric, sew the center back seam up to within 3" of the top. Press the seam allowances open and topstitch around the opening.

**11.** Gather all four layers of netting at one time along one long edge to fit the bodice. Right sides together, sew the gathered netting overskirt to the bodice.

**12.** Gather the top edge of the satin skirt to fit the bodice. Right sides together, with the netting overskirt in between, sew the satin skirt to the bodice. Zigzag the seam allowances to prevent raveling.

**13.** Stitch the ½"-wide trim along the waistline.

**14.** Lapping the right over the left about ¼", sew three snaps to the center back opening of the bodice.

## Headband

**1.** Cut the pipe cleaner to 7½" long. Fold the ends under ½".

**2.** Cut two 1¼" x 16" strips of netting. Layer

them and gather them together along one long edge so that it measures 3½" long. Hot glue the gathered netting to the middle of the pipe cleaner headband.

**3.** Hot glue fabric roses over the glued netting and pipe cleaner. Bend to fit doll's head.

## Magic Wand

Pattern piece 30

**1.** Cut one star of heavy interfacing and one of scrap silver fabric. Use a glue stick to adhere the wrong side of the silver fabric star to the interfacing star. Use tacky glue around the edge of the star to attach sequin trim.

**2.** Paint the dowel with silver and glitter paint. Hot glue the star on one end of the dowel.

**3.** Tie two colors of ribbon (we used blue and silver) in a bow around the wand.

# Little Red Riding Hood

# Granny's Cottage Setting

Granny's bedroom is furnished with old-fashioned comfy touches. Her bed is constructed like Baby Bear's in Goldilocks, but it has an upholstered look. The featherbed is just like a mattress, but fluffier.

## Supplies:

Cardboard project display board, 48" x 36"
1⅓ yd. cream felt for walls
2 sheets white foam board, 20" x 30" x ⅜"
1½ yd. fabric to cover bed
1⅔ yd. gathered eyelet edging (3"-wide) for dust ruffle
¾ yd. fabric for featherbed
Fiberfill to stuff featherbed and pillow
⅔ yd. fabric for quilt back and pillow
Thin batting for quilt, 21" x 24"
Fabric for quilt top, 21" x 24"
¾ yd. fabric for curtains
1 yd. velvet ribbon (⅞"-wide) for tiebacks
Medium woven interfacing, 4½" x 6", for sampler
Embroidery floss
Bias tape for sampler frame
1 skein variegated worsted weight yarn
Size I crochet hook
Hot glue gun
Spray adhesive
Craft glue stick
Utility knife

*Note:* For the furniture sewing, use ½" seam allowances to make them a little more durable.

## Setting

Pattern piece 31

**1.** Cut the cream felt to fit the display board plus about 1" extra around all sides. Following the manufacturer's instructions, spray adhesive sparingly over the entire front of the display board. Let it dry a bit before you attempt to lay the felt out on it because if it is too wet, it can spot the felt. Stretch the felt out over the board, working out any bubbles with your fingers. You can usually lift the felt up carefully and reposition it if necessary. Use a glue stick to secure any loose edges. Trim away excess fabric around the cardboard edges.

**2.** Cut two 13" x 26" curtains. These curtains are just props, so there's no need to hem each edge twice. Hem the long edges by pressing them under ¼" and stitching. Press the lower edges under 1" and stitch. Make casings by pressing the top edges under 3", then stitching 1" from the edge and again at 2" from the edge.

**3.** Make a curtain rod from a ¾" x 14" scrap of foam board or rigid cardboard. Slide the curtains onto it. Use a dab of hot glue to secure the open ends of the curtain casings to the curtain rod. Hot glue the back side of the curtain rod directly on the felt wall at a pleasing height. Cut the velvet ribbon in half and use each half as a tieback.

**4.** Using a pencil or washout marker, copy HOME SWEET HOME on the interfacing (pattern piece #31). Cross-stitch the words. Glue pieces of bias tape around the interfacing to form a frame. Glue stick or hot glue the sampler in place on the felt wall.

**5.** We used 1½ yd. of tan felt for the floor in this scene, but there's no need for a special fabric. Children will use whatever is available in their rooms for carpet or flooring.

## Bed

**1.** Cut two 12" x 22½" pieces of foam board for the top and bottom of the bed frame. Cut two 4½" x 22½" pieces for the sides of the bed frame and two 4½" x 11½" pieces for the ends of the bed frame.

**2.** Cut one 12" x 11" piece for the headboard and one 12" x 7" piece for the foot board. Make a paper template to cut uniformly round corners on the headboard and foot board.

**3.** Using the glue gun, glue the corners of the bed frame as shown.

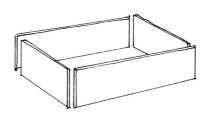

**4.** Quickly apply glue to one side of the frame along the narrow edges and attach the bed bottom piece. When cool, apply glue to the other side of the frame along the edges and attach the bed top piece.

**5.** Wrap fabric around the top, long sides, and bottom of the box you have just created. Cut it so it is about ½" larger than the surfaces to be covered. Wrap the raw edges around and glue stick them in place.

**6.** To "upholster" the headboard and foot board, place them on the wrong side of the bed frame fabric and trace around each, adding ¼" seam allowance all the way around. Cut two for the headboard and two for the foot board.

**7.** Right sides together, stitch around the curved edges of the foot board and headboard covers. Leave the straight edge open. Turn right side out and press.

**8.** Rub glue stick all over both sides of the foot board. Carefully pull the foot board cover over it and smooth the fabric. Repeat with the headboard. Glue the open edges shut.

**9.** Hot glue the eyelet edging to the top edges of the bed sides, extending the ends around to the head and foot of the bed by about 1". This will be hidden later.

**10.** Generously hot glue the headboard and foot board to the respective ends of the bed.

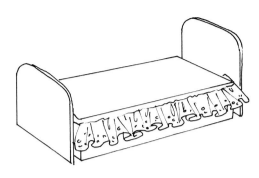

# Featherbed

**1.** Cut two 14½" x 25" pieces of featherbed fabric. Right sides together, sew around all four sides, leaving a 5" opening at one short end for turning and stuffing.

**2.** Turn the featherbed right side out, press, and stuff with fiberfill to the desired firmness. Hand stitch the opening closed.

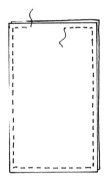

## Pillow

**1.** Cut two 6" x 9" rectangles of pillow fabric. Right sides together, sew around three sides, leaving one short end open. Turn right side out, press, and stuff with fiberfill.

**2.** Tuck the raw edges of the opening ½" into the pillow. Tuck in a 6" length of eyelet edging, turning the ends under ½", and machine stitch across the open end.

## Quilt

**1.** This is a generously wide quilt. Cut out a quilt top 24" wide and 21" long. Cut out a quilt backing the same size.

**2.** Make a "quilt sandwich," layering from the bottom up, first the batting, then the quilt top right side up, then the backing right side down. Stitch around all four sides, leaving a 5" opening to turn. Turn right side out, press, and hand stitch the opening closed.

## Crocheted Afghan

Children tend to use whatever is available for props in their plays. A purchased dishcloth could make a reasonable doll-size afghan, and a hand crocheted one found at a church bazaar would be even better. But if you can crochet on a rudimentary level, you can make this afghan yourself, as long as you know the following stitches: chain, single, double, and treble. Don't worry about a gauge, because it really doesn't matter what size your creation ends up.

Ch 48.

Row 1: Sc in second ch from hook and in each ch across. 47 sc.
Row 2: Ch 1, turn; sc in first sc, (tr in next sc, sc in next sc) across.
Row 3: Ch 1, turn; sc in each st across.
Row 4: Ch 4 (counts as first dc plus ch 1), turn; skip next sc, (ch 1, skip next sc, dc in next sc) across.
Row 5: Ch 1, turn; sc in each dc and in each ch-1 space across.

Repeat Rows 2 through 5 eight times.
Repeat Rows 3 and 3 once more. Break off yarn.

Fringes: Add a fringe to every other sc in the beginning row and ending row of the afghan as follows: Cut two 3" pieces of yarn for each fringe. Pull both pieces through the sc with your crochet hook, then pull the ends of the yarn through the loop and tug on them to secure the fringe.

# Little Red Riding Hood

This is a typical Black Forest fairy tale outfit: blouse, dirndle skirt, lace-up vest, and apron. Lengthened and made of green wool, the hooded cape would be perfect for a traditional Irish folk tale as well.

*The model is a Götz doll.*

# Supplies:

**Blouse**
$^1/_3$ yd. white batiste
16" flat eyelet edging (1"-wide)
9" elastic ($^1/_8$"-wide)
3 snaps or 3" Velcro strip
**Skirt**
$^1/_3$ yd. striped cotton
1 hook and eye or Velcro dot
**Vest**
$^1/_4$ yd. broadcloth
20" satin ribbon ($^1/_8$"-wide)
3 snaps or 3" Velcro strip
**Apron**
$^1/_3$ yd. print fabric
**Hooded Cape**
$^2/_3$ yd. red wool fabric
$^2/_3$ yd. matching lining
30" red ribbon ($^1/_4$"-wide)
**Basket**
Small basket and cloth scrap
Brown polymer clay for bread in basket
Assorted miniature goodies for basket
Hot glue gun

# Blouse

Pattern pieces 15, 16, 17

**1.** Cut one blouse front, two backs, and two sleeves from the white batiste. Right sides together, sew the front to the back at the shoulder seams.
**2.** Press the center back openings $^1/_8$" toward the wrong side. Press under another $^1/_8$" and stitch.

**3.** Gather the flat eyelet to fit the neckline, with the short ends turned under $^1/_4$". With

the wrong side of the eyelet to the right side of the blouse, baste in place.
**4.** To finish off the neckline, cut a 1" x 8$^3/_4$" bias strip from the batiste and pin it to the blouse so that one long edge is flush with the neckline and the short ends extend $^1/_4$" beyond the center backs. Stitch in place.
**5.** Grade seam allowances. Tucking in the short ends, fold the bias over twice and slip-stitch to the inside of the neckline.

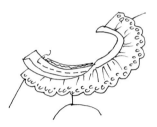

**6.** Zigzag or serge the bottom edge of each sleeve, then turn it up and stitch by machine (or use your rolled hem attachment for a nice hem).
**7.** Cut the elastic in half. Using a pencil, draw a line on the wrong side of the sleeve $^3/_4$" above and parallel to the hemmed sleeve bottom. Using two or three straight stitches, anchor one end of the elastic to the fabric on the line. Switch to a wide enough zigzag stitch to swing back and forth over the elastic, creating a mini-casing. Stretch the elastic as you proceed to the end of the line; straight stitch the elastic to the fabric to anchor it at the end.

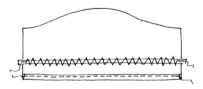

**8.** Gather the caps of the sleeves between *s on the pattern piece. Right sides together, stitch the sleeve to the blouse armhole.

Only then will you sew the underarm seam, starting at the bottom of the sleeve and ending at the lower edge of the blouse.

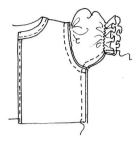

**9.** Hem the bottom of the blouse by turning it under ¼" twice and stitching. Sew snaps or a Velcro strip to the center backs, overlapping the right over the left by about ¼".

## Skirt

**1.** Cut a 8½" x 45" rectangle from the skirt fabric. Cut a 1½" x 12½" waistband on grain.
**2.** Press one long edge of the skirt under ¼". Press it under another ¼" and stitch.
**3.** Right sides together, sew the center back seam up to within 3" of the unhemmed edge (the waist edge). Press the seam allowances open. Topstitch around the opening to finish it off.

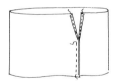

**4.** Gather the top edge of the skirt to fit the waistband, with the waistband extending beyond the skirt by ¼" on each end. Pin the right side of the waistband to the wrong side of the skirt. Stitch.
**5.** Press the remaining long edge of the waistband under ¼". Fold it over so it ends up on the right side of the skirt, tucking in the short ends. Topstitch from the right side of the skirt.

**6.** Lapping the right center back over the left by about ¼" (or however much you need to for your particular doll), sew the hook and eye or Velcro to the waistband.

## Vest

Pattern pieces 18, 19

**1.** This lined vest laces up the front, but it also has a back opening so kids don't have to unlace the vest to change clothes. Cut out four backs and four fronts from the vest broadcloth.
**2.** Right sides together, stitch each back to a front at the shoulder seams so you have a vest and a lining in four parts. Press.
**3.** Right sides together, pin left and right vest parts to left and right lining parts and stitch up the center fronts, around the neckline, and down the center backs. Sew the armholes.

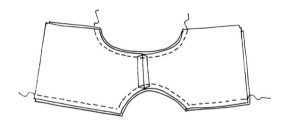

**4.** Stitch the side seams together by opening up the vest and lining at the side seams. Turn to the right side and press.

**5.** Press the bottom edges of both vests and linings ¼" toward the inside. Stitch the opening closed.

**6.** With a large-eyed needle, thread the ribbon and lace the vest fronts together, following the dots on the pattern piece. Tie the ends together at the bottom edge.

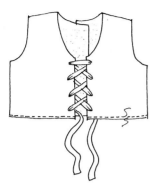

**7.** Sew snaps or Velcro to the center backs of the vest, lapping the right over the left approximately ¼".

## Apron

**1.** Cut a 6" x 15" rectangle from the apron fabric. Cut a 1½" x 6½" waistband on grain. Cut two 1½" x 22" ties.
**2.** Hem one long edge and both short ends of the rectangle by pressing it under ¼" and topstitching. Gather the remaining long edge to fit the waistband, with the waistband extending beyond the gathered apron ¼" on each end.
**3.** Pin the right side of the waistband to the wrong side of the apron, then stitch. Press the remaining long edge of the waistband under ¼". Set aside.

**4.** Narrow hem the long edges of each tie, either with your rolled hem attachment or by pressing it under ⅛" twice and stitching. Fold one end of each tie toward the wrong side at a 45° angle. Stitch. Cut off the excess fabric.
**5.** On the remaining short ends of the ties, make a pleat and pin it ½" inside where the waistband seam will be. Tuck in the short ends of the waistband ¼" on each end and enclose the pleated ends of the ties by folding the waistband over to the right side of the apron. Topstitch all three sides of the waistband. Wrap the ties around to the front of the doll and tie.

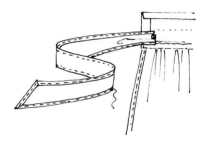

## Hooded Cape
### Pattern pieces 32, 33

**1.** Cut out two capes from the wool and two from the lining. Cut two hoods each from the wool and lining.
**2.** Right sides together, sew the center back seam of the cape. Repeat for the lining.
**3.** Pin the lining to the cape, right sides together. Stitch down one center front, around the lower edge of the cape, and back up the remaining center front. Trim the corners of the seam allowances, turn right side out, and carefully press through a cloth.

**4.** Make three evenly spaced pleats along the neckline on each side of the center back so the neckline measures 12¼". Both the wool and lining fabric should be pleated together as though it were one layer. Baste.

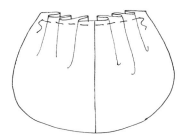

**5.** Right sides together, sew the long curved seam of the hood. Repeat for the hood lining.
**6.** Right sides together, pin the hood lining to the hood and stitch around the face edge. Turn right side out.
**7.** Gather the neck edge of the hood to fit the pleated neckline of the cape. Right sides together, stitch the hood to the cape. Zigzag or serge the seam allowance to finish it. Press the seam allowance down toward the cape.

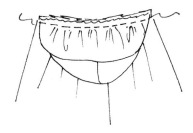

**8.** Cut the ribbon in half. Fold one end under ½" and stitch over the neckline seam as shown. Repeat for the other tie.

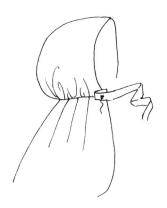

# Red Riding Hood's Basket of Goodies

**1.** Line the basket with the scrap of cloth. Following the manufacturer's instructions, mold bread loaves from polymer clay. You can make other fruits and foodstuffs from other colors of clay or find miniature ones already made at a craft store.
**2.** Hot glue the goodies into the basket for safekeeping. (You don't want the Big Bad Wolf to get them too easily.)
*Note:* These tiny items would not, of course, be suitable for young children.

# Granny

This nightgown and cap pattern could be used for everyday, as well as for acting out other fairy tales. How about the "Princess and the Pea?"

*The model is an Engelpuppen doll.*

## Supplies:

1 yd. flannel
1¹⁄₃ yd. flat eyelet edging (³⁄₄"-wide)
7" elastic (¹⁄₈"-wide)
2 snaps
2 buttons (¹⁄₄")
1 yd. bias tape for cap
12½" elastic for cap (¹⁄₄"-wide)

## Nightgown

Pattern pieces 23, 34, 35, 36, 37

**1.** Cut two back yokes, four front yokes, two collars, and two sleeves from the flannel. Cut two 9" x 10" rectangles for the front skirt and one 18" x 10" for the back skirt. Cut two ruffle pieces 3" x 18" and one 3" x 36".
**2.** Right sides together, sew one back yoke to two front yokes. Repeat for the lining.

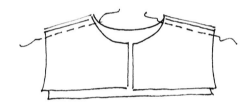

**3.** Cut a 28" piece of eyelet edging and gather it to the outside curved edge of the collar. Right sides together, sew the eyelet to the collar.

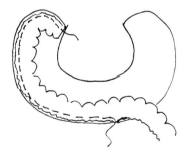

**4.** Right sides together, sew the collar lining to the collar with the eyelet in between. Leave the neckline edge unstitched. Turn right side out and press.
**5.** Pin the collar to the right side of the night-gown yoke. Note that the collar doesn't go all the way to the center front edges of the night-gown. Baste.

**6.** Pin the yoke lining over the yoke, right sides together, and stitch around the neckline and down the center fronts. Clip the corners, trim the seams, and turn right side out. Press.

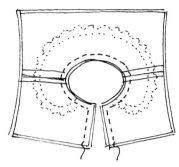

**7.** Baste the shoulder seam edges of the lining and the nightgown together.
**8.** Narrow hem one long edge of each ruffle piece. Gather the remaining long edge of each.
**9.** Right sides together, sew the 36" ruffle to the 18" wide skirt (the back) and the 18" ruffles to each 9" wide skirt (the fronts).
**10.** Right sides together, sew the center front seam of the nightgown skirt, starting at the bottom of the ruffle and ending 3" from the top. Press the seam allowance open and stitch around the opening.

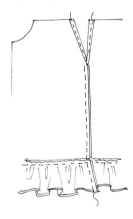

**11.** Using the armhole guide (pattern piece #36), cut out two armholes at the top of the 18" wide back skirt. Cut one armhole in each front skirt. Gather the top of each skirt piece to fit the yokes.
**12.** Right sides together, sew the lined back yoke to the back skirt and the lined front yokes to the skirt fronts, lining up the armholes.

**13.** Cut the remainder of the eyelet in half. Gather each piece and sew it, right sides together, to the bottom edge of each sleeve. Press open.

**14.** Cut the ⅛" elastic in half. Using a pencil, draw a line on the wrong side of the sleeve ¾" above and parallel to the hemmed sleeve bottom. Using two or three straight stitches, anchor one end of the elastic to the fabric on the line. Switch to a wide enough zigzag stitch to swing back and forth over the elastic, creating a mini-casing. Stretch the elastic as you proceed to the end of the line; straight stitch the elastic to the fabric to anchor it at the end.

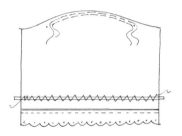

**15.** Gather the caps of the sleeves between *s on the pattern piece. Right sides together, stitch the sleeves to the nightgown armholes.

**16.** Sew the underarm seams from the wrist to the ruffle.

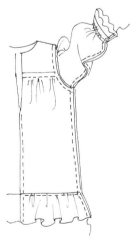

**17.** Sew two decorative buttons to the yoke front on the right center front. Sew snaps underneath.

# Granny's Nightcap

Pattern piece 38

**1.** Cut one nightcap from flannel. Narrow hem the outside edge.

**2.** Pin bias tape 1" from the edge of the circle and stitch it in place to the wrong side of the fabric, stitching along both edges of the tape. The ends of the tape should be turned under and just meet. Do not stitch down the short ends.

**3.** Thread elastic through the casing and secure with a few stitches.

# Big Bad Wolf Mask

In this case, a doll must portray not only Granny, but the Big Bad Wolf as well. Look at those big white teeth!

## Supplies:

Scraps of felt in the following colors: charcoal, gray, black, white, red
2/3 yd. ribbon
Craft glue stick

## Wolf Mask

Pattern pieces 39, 40, 41, 42, 43, 44, 45

**1.** Cut out one wolf face and one snout from charcoal felt. Cut out one overlay and one snout from gray felt. Cut out two ears from charcoal and two from gray. Cut out a tongue from red, a nose from black, and two sets of teeth from white felt.

**2.** Glue the gray overlay on top of the charcoal face, lining up the eye holes. Glue (sparingly) the two colors of snout together, with just a little glue around the edges. Sparingly glue each gray ear to a charcoal ear. Be sure to make a right and a left. Let these pieces dry completely.

**3.** Pin the darts in the layered snout. Stitch through both layers.

**4.** Right sides together, stitch the snout to the face of the mask.

**5.** Stitch the black nose to the end of the snout and the teeth to each side of the snout.

**6.** Stitch the tongue through both layers of the face mask where indicated on the pattern piece.

**7.** Fold each ear along the line indicated on the pattern piece so the charcoal layer is on the outside of each ear. Stitch in place through both layers of the mask.

**8.** Cut the ribbon in half and stitch each piece where indicated on the sides of the mask. Be sure to fold the end of the ribbon under ½" where you attach it to the mask.

# Hansel & Gretel

# Gingerbread House in the Black Forest Setting

This setting can work double duty. If you don't glue the gingerbread house and men in place, you can use the forest scene when playing Wizard of Oz or other common folk tales set in the deep, dark woods. Don't forget to have the Gingerbread Witch offer a candy cane or other sweet treat to Hansel.

## Supplies:

Cardboard project display board, 48" x 36"
1⅓ yd. deep blue felt for Black Forest sky
  Optional: 1½ yd. grass or fern print fabric
  for foreground
Scraps of brown and green print fabrics for
  tree trunks and leafy branches
Scraps of variegated green fabrics for grass
  and ground
Fat quarter of red brick print fabric for oven
  and chimney
Scrap of black felt for oven door
Cardboard box approximately 8" x 8" x 6" for
  oven
⅓ yd. cinnamon colored felt for gingerbread
  house and men
1 square white felt for frosting roof
Scraps of red and white striped fabric for
  house trim
Scrap of pink broadcloth for door
½ yd. red satin ribbon (⅜"-wide) for window
8" red grosgrain ribbon (¼"-wide) for window
Scrap of contrasting brown broadcloth for
  windowpanes
5 ceramic buttons painted like peppermint
  candies
6 ceramic buttons painted like mint leaf
  candies
Red heart-shaped sequins
Button or small circle of felt for doorknob
Hot glue gun
Spray adhesive
Craft glue stick

## Setting

Pattern pieces  46,  47,  48,  49,  50,  51,
52,  53,  54,  55,  56

**1.** Following the manufacturer's instructions, spray adhesive sparingly over the entire front of the display board. Let it dry a bit before you stretch the felt over the board, working out any bubbles with your fingers. Trim away excess felt along the cardboard edges.
**2.** Cut out simple grass yard shapes and use spray adhesive to apply them to the background. Cut out a tree trunk and leaf clusters and glue the Black Forest in place.
**3.** Make the gingerbread house as a separate removable piece. Because it is made of felt, it will stick to the felt background while in use. First cut out a gingerbread house from the cinnamon felt. Next cut out the snow roof pieces from white felt and use spray adhesive to attach them to the house.
**4.** Using the photograph and your imagination, embellish the house with whatever you can find. Cut out the door from pink broadcloth and the window for the door (pattern piece #53) from brown fabric. Cut a larger window for the house (3½" x 2½") from brown fabric and trim it with red ribbon. When using ceramic buttons as trim, be sure to use hot glue because the buttons are too heavy for a glue stick or spray adhesive.
**5.** Cut out two gingerbread men from the cinnamon felt and glue heart sequin buttons to them. The gingerbread men may be left as separate removable pieces in case you want to rearrange things or act out a different fairy tale.
**6.** To make the oven, wrap the small cardboard box with red brick printed fabric as though you were wrapping a package, tucking in all ends neatly. Secure with a glue stick. Cut out an oven door from black felt and glue in place.

# Gretel

European folk wear is always colorful and fun to make. Gretel's skirt is quite simple and opens all the way in the back, for quick costume changes.

*The model is an Apple Valley Friends doll.*

## Supplies:

¼ yd. navy broadcloth for blouse
9" elastic (⅛"-wide)
¼ yd. red flannel for jacket
¼ yd. red batiste for jacket lining
1¼ yd. embroidered ribbon for jacket (⅜"-wide)
⅓ yd. multi-colored stripe fabric for skirt
⅓ yd. white batiste for apron
Scraps of brown fabric and white organdy for pockets
1 yd. red braided trim for apron
3" Velcro strip
1 hook and eye
Red and black embroidery floss

## Blouse

Pattern pieces 15, 16, 17

**1.** From the navy fabric, cut out one front and two backs. Right sides together, sew the shoulder seams.
**2.** Press the center back openings under ⅛". Press under another ⅛" and stitch.
**3.** Cut a bias strip of navy fabric 1" x 8¾". Pin it to the neckline of the blouse so one long edge is flush with the neckline and the short ends extend ¼" beyond the center backs. Stitch in place.
**4.** Grade the seam allowances. Tucking in the short ends, fold the bias over twice and slipstitch.
**5.** Cut out two sleeves. Zigzag or serge the lower edge of each sleeve, then turn them under and machine stitch (or use your machine's rolled hem attachment).

**6.** Cut the elastic in half. Using a pencil, draw a line on the wrong side of the sleeve ¾" above and parallel to the hemmed sleeve bottom. Using two or three straight stitches, anchor one end of the elastic to the fabric on the line. Switch to a wide enough zigzag stitch to swing back and forth over the elastic, creating a mini-casing. Stretch the elastic as you proceed to the end of the line; straight stitch the elastic to the fabric to anchor it at the end.

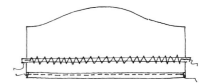

**7.** Gather the sleeve caps between *s on the pattern piece. Right sides together, stitch each sleeve to a blouse armhole.

**8.** Right sides together, sew the underarm seam from the lower sleeve to the bottom of the blouse.

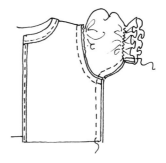

**9.** Hem the bottom of the blouse by turning it under ¼" twice and stitching. Sew the Velcro strip to the center backs, lapping the right over the left about ¼".

## Dirndl Skirt

**1.** Cut a rectangle of the striped fabric 8½" x 45". Leave the selvages intact, as they will be

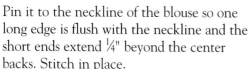

at the center back of the skirt. Cut a waistband of the same fabric 1½" x 12½".

**2.** Press under one long edge of the skirt ¼". Press it under another ¼" and stitch.

**3.** Press the center back edges of the skirt under ¼". Stitch.

**4.** Gather the remaining long edge of the skirt and pull the gathering threads until the waist edge measures 11¼".

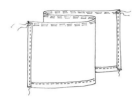

Pin the right side of the waistband to the wrong side of the skirt waist, with the waistband extending ¼" beyond the skirt on the right center back and ½" on the left center back. Stitch.

**5.** Press the unstitched long edge of the waistband under ¼". Fold the waistband over to the right side of the skirt and topstitch in place, tucking in the short ends ¼". Stitch a hook and eye in place so the short end of the waistband overlaps the long one.

## Apron

Pattern piece 57

**1.** Cut a 6" x 16" rectangle from the white batiste. Hem the short sides of the apron by turning them under ¼" twice and stitching.

**2.** Cut a 2" x 40" strip of batiste on grain for the ruffle. Fold it in half

lengthwise and stitch the short ends. Turn right side out and press. Gather the long raw edges of the ruffle. Right sides together, stitch the ruffle to the bottom of the apron.

**3.** Cut out two 3" x 3" squares of batiste for the pockets. Cut out two gingerbread men (pattern piece #57) from the brown fabric scraps. Cut out two 3" x 3" squares of organdy.

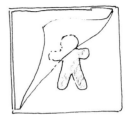

**4.** Make sandwiches of the gingerbread men between the batiste and organdy squares. You should see the gingerbread men through the organdy. Pin securely.

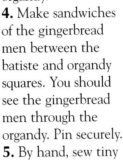

**5.** By hand, sew tiny running stitches with brown thread around the gingerbread men, encasing them in the white fabric. Stitch very close to each figure. Using two strands of black floss, make two-wrap French knots for eyes. With two strands of red floss, make three two-wrap French knots for buttons.

**6.** Hem the top of the pockets by turning the fabric under ⅛" twice and stitching. Press under the remaining three sides ¼" and pin the pockets to the apron so their edges are 1¼" from the apron's center and 2" up from the ruffle. Stitch around the three folded edges.

**7.** Sew one row of braided trim 1" above the ruffle and one row ½" above the first row.

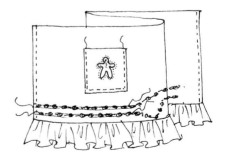

**8.** To make a waistband, cut a 1½" x 6½" piece of batiste on grain. Gather the top of the apron to fit the waistband and pin the wrong side of the apron to it, letting the waistband extend beyond the gathered apron $\frac{1}{4}$" on each side. Stitch in place and set aside.

**9.** To make the apron ties, cut two $1\frac{1}{2}$" x 18" pieces of batiste. Fold over the long edges $\frac{1}{4}$" (or use your rolled hem attachment) and stitch. Fold one short end of each tie at a 45° angle so the short edge is flush with the long edge. Stitch down. Fold out to the right side. On the remaining short end of the ties, make a pleat and pin it $\frac{1}{2}$" inside where the waistband seam will be.

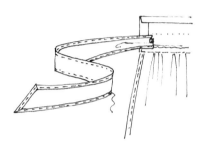

**10.** Press the long edge of the waistband $\frac{1}{4}$" toward the wrong side. Tucking in the short ends of the waistband $\frac{1}{4}$" and enclosing the ties, fold the waistband over to the right side and topstitch all three sides.

## Jacket

Pattern pieces 58, 59, 60

**1.** Cut out two fronts, one back, and two sleeves from the flannel. Cut out two fronts and one back from the lining fabric.
**2.** Mark and sew the back darts in both the jacket and its lining.
**3.** Right sides together, sew the jacket fronts to the back at the shoulder seams. Repeat for the lining.

**4.** Right sides together, sew the jacket to its lining by stitching around the neckline, down both center fronts and across the lower edge of the fronts. Stitch across the lower edge of the back also. Clip curves and turn right side out. Press.

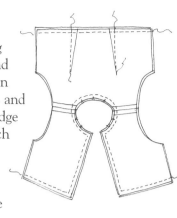

**5.** Baste the jacket and its lining together around the armholes to prevent slip-ups when sewing in the sleeves.
**6.** Press the front edge on the fold line at the neckline as shown on the pattern piece to create a lapel effect. Set aside.
**7.** Hem the jacket sleeves by pressing them under $\frac{1}{4}$" and stitching. Cover the hem with embroidered ribbon and either zigzag or hand stitch it in place.

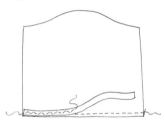

**8.** Right sides together, sew the jacket sleeves to the armholes. Sew the side seams of the jacket and the lining as one unit.

**9.** Sew embroidered ribbon around the hem, up the center fronts, and around the neckline in the same manner you trimmed the sleeve hems.

# Hansel

This costume was designed for us by our friend, Marlene Ford. Marlene originally came to Duluth from Germany, and she is a wealth of information about German folk costumes.

*The model is an Apple Valley Friends doll.*

## Supplies:

**Shirt**
1/3 yd. red check fabric
4 buttons (1/4")
4 snaps

**Knickers**
1/4 yd. vinyl, Ultrasuede, or leather
16" braid (5/8"-wide) for suspenders
12 eyelets (1/4")
Eyelet installing tool
20" cord for lacing
11" elastic (1/8")
11 1/2" elastic (1/4"-wide)
4 buttons (3/8")

**Hat**
1/4 yd. green felt
15" braid (3/8"-wide)
Decorative feather
5/8" fancy button

## Shirt

Pattern pieces 61, 62, 63, 64

**1.** Cut out four fronts, two backs, two sleeves, and one collar.
**2.** Right sides together, sew two fronts to one back at the shoulder seams. Repeat to make the lining. Press the seam allowances open.
**3.** Right sides together, fold the collar in half lengthwise. Stitch the short ends. Clip the corners, trim the seams, and turn right side out. Press.
**4.** Right sides together, pin the collar to the shirt, centering it on the neckline. Note that the collar doesn't go all the way to the center front edges of the shirt.
**5.** Right sides together, pin the shirt lining to the shirt with the collar in between. Stitch around the neckline and down the center fronts. Clip the curves, turn right side out, and press. Baste the lining to the shirt around the armholes.

**6.** Hem the lower edges of the sleeves by pressing them under 1/4" twice and stitching.

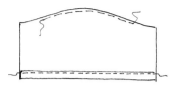

**7.** Right sides together, pin the sleeves to the shirt armholes, easing the sleeve caps. Stitch.
**8.** Sew the underarm seam from the bottom of the sleeve to the waist of the shirt.
**9.** To finish the lower edge of the shirt, zigzag stitch, press it 1/4" toward the wrong side, and stitch.

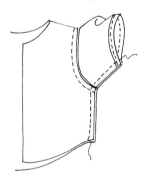

**10.** Lapping the left front over the right about 1/4", sew snaps to the center front, placing the first one at the neck edge and spacing the rest 1" apart. Sew decorative buttons to the left front over the snaps.

## Knickers

Pattern pieces 65, 66, 67

**1.** Cut out two pants, two back suspender tabs, and four front suspender tabs from the leather-like (or leather) material.
*Note:* Pinning vinyl, Ultrasuede, or leather can be difficult and the pinholes will be there forever. We recommend you use a removable cellophane tape made especially for sewing such materials to keep the parts together as you sew.
**2.** Right sides together, sew the center front and center back seams.
**3.** Install six eyelets on each pant leg where indicated on the pattern piece.
**4.** Turn the bottom leg edges under 3/8" and stitch to form a casing. Using a tapestry needle or bodkin, thread 5 1/2" of the 1/8" elastic

through the casing of each leg and secure the ends with a few stitches.

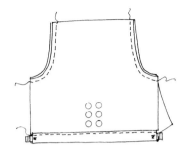

**5.** Sew the inner leg seam.

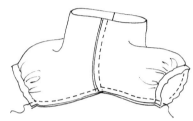

**6.** To make the waistline casing, fold the waistline edge ½" toward the inside of the garment and stitch around, leaving an opening at the center back to insert the elastic. Thread the ¼" elastic through the casing and secure the ends with a few stitches.

**7.** Cut the braid in half to make two suspenders. Tape two front suspender tabs together, right sides out, with one suspender tucked inside the top of the tab ¼" as shown. Topstitch around all edges of the tab, anchoring the suspender in the tab. Repeat with the second front suspender tab.

**8.** Tape the two halves of the back suspender tab together, inserting both the remaining ends of the suspender braid into them. Topstitch around the back tab as you did the front ones.

**9.** Tuck the back suspender tab about ¾" down into the center back waist of the knickers. Topstitch to secure the suspender tab.

**10.** Cut buttonholes as marked on the front suspender tab pattern piece. Sew two buttons on each side of the knickers front as marked on the pattern piece. Button the front suspender tabs to the pants.

**11.** Lace the cording through the eyelets and tie at the knees.

## Hat

Pattern pieces 68, 69

**1.** Cut one brim and one crown from the felt. Stitch the back seam of the crown, right sides together.

**2.** Pin the crown to the brim, right sides together, and stitch. Pin the seam allowance to the inside of the crown and topstitch.

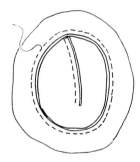

**3.** Pin the braid to the seam over the topstitching and hand sew in place. Be sure to tuck the raw ends of the braid under to keep them from fraying.

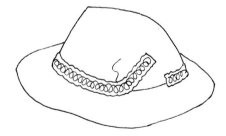

**4.** Stitch or glue the feather to the left side of the hat crown. Sew the fancy button over it.

# Gingerbread Witch

Although we call her a witch, this character is often called an old crone or an old hag. Basically, she was probably just a peculiar old woman who frightened little children.

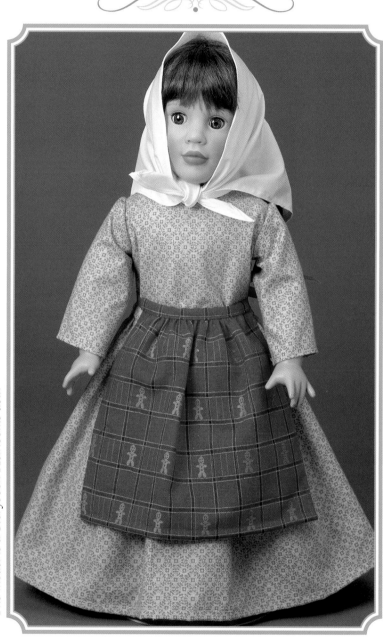

*The model is a Storybook Heirlooms doll.*

## Supplies:

$2/3$ yd. dress fabric
$1/4$ yd. apron fabric
16" square scarf fabric
1 yd. grosgrain ribbon ($3/8$"-wide) to match apron
3 snaps

## Dress

Pattern pieces 70, 71, 72

**1.** Cut two front bodices, four back bodices, and two sleeves from the dress fabric. This dress bodice is self-lined.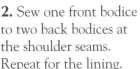

**2.** Sew one front bodice to two back bodices at the shoulder seams. Repeat for the lining.

**3.** Pin the bodice to its lining, right sides together, and stitch up one center back, around the neckline, and down the other center back. Trim the seams, turn right side out, and press.

**4.** Hem the bottom edges of both sleeves by pressing them under $1/4$" and topstitching.

**5.** Gather the sleeve caps and pin them to the lined bodice armholes, right sides together. Stitch.

**6.** Right sides together, sew the underarm seams from wrist to waist.

**7.** Cut a 10" x 38" rectangle of the dress fabric. Right sides together, sew the center back seam up to within 3" of the top. Press the seam allowances open. Topstitch around the opening.

**8.** Hem the lower edge of the skirt by pressing it under $1/4$" and then another $1/4$". Stitch.

**9.** Gather the top edge of the skirt to fit the bodice, right sides together. Stitch.

**10.** Lapping the right over the left about $1/4$", sew three snaps to the center back opening of the bodice.

## Apron

**1.** Cut an apron 9" x $7½$". Cut a waistband $1¼$" x 5".

**2.** Press all but one 9" edge of the apron under $1/4$" and topstitch to hem.

**3.** Gather the remaining 9" edge to fit the waistband. The waistband should extend beyond the edges of the apron by $1/4$" on each end, and the right side of the waistband should be pinned to the wrong side of the apron. Stitch.

**4.** Fold the remaining edge of the waistband under $1/4$" and fold it over to the right side of the apron. Pin it in place, tucking in the short ends of the waistband. Cut the ribbon in half and tuck each tie into the waistband about $½$". Topstitch the ends of the waistband to anchor the ties and continue stitching along the waistband to enclose the apron in it.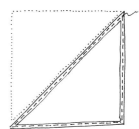

## Scarf

**1.** Fold the 16" square of fabric in half to form a triangle and cut along the $23½$" long fold. Discard one fabric triangle.

**2.** Narrow hem all three sides. Tie under the doll's chin.

# Alice in Wonderland

# Wonderland Setting

There are, of course, many scenes in this story that would be fun to act out. We chose the "Off with her head!" wacky croquet game and squeezed in a tea party for good measure. The Cheshire Cat absolutely had to make an appearance. Try to see things in a new way (like through a looking glass) and find things around the house to play with. After we shot this picture, we realized that we have a string of novelty lights featuring doll-size flamingos, which the Queen of Hearts preferred over the standard mallets. And if you find a small hedgehog curled up around your house, put it to work!

Incidentally, the croquet set shown does require a saw and a drill, so if you have a tool-free home, you might want to look for those flamingo lights.

## Supplies:

Cardboard project display board, 48" x 36"
$1\frac{1}{3}$ yd. sky blue felt for background
$1\frac{1}{2}$ yd. green felt for foreground
Scraps of brown and green print fabrics for
    trees and shrubs
$\frac{2}{3}$ yd. stone or brick printed fabric for castle
Scraps of gray and white felt for Cheshire Cat
    and castle windows
Scraps of foam board and woodgrain adhesive
    vinyl covering or fabric for table
Handkerchief for tablecloth
Wooden dowel, $\frac{3}{8}$"-diameter
Wooden dowel, 1"-diameter
4 wooden balls $1\frac{1}{4}$"-diameter
Medium gauge wire for wickets
Black, yellow, red, and green acrylic paints and
    brush
Doll-size tea set
Hot glue gun
Spray adhesive
Craft glue stick
Utility knife

## Setting

Pattern pieces 46, 47, 73, 74

**1.** Following the manufacturer's instructions, spray adhesive sparingly over the entire front of the display board. Let it dry a bit before you stretch the felt over the board, working out any bubbles with your fingers. Trim away excess felt along the cardboard edges.
**2.** Cut out a simple castle shape and use spray adhesive to apply it to the background. Cut out a tree trunk and leaf clusters and glue them in place. Add shrubs and castle windows as you please.
**3.** Cut out the Cheshire Cat from gray felt and his teeth from white felt. Using a permanent marker, draw lines as shown on the teeth. Add features with marker to the gray cat face. Glue the teeth to the face and the face to the tree branch.

## Table

**1.** Use the utility knife to cut four 4" x $6\frac{1}{2}$" sides of the table from the foam board. Cut a circle approximately 7" in diameter by tracing around a small plate or other circular object, or cut a 7" square for the tabletop.
**2.** Hot glue the corners of the table together so you have a square pedestal $6\frac{1}{2}$" tall. Cover all four sides with wood-grained adhesive vinyl.
**3.** Apply hot glue to the top edges of the pedestal and place the tabletop on top. Add the handkerchief tablecloth and tea set.

## Croquet Set

**1.** Wooden dowels can be purchased at hardware stores and craft stores. The wooden balls and acrylic paints can be found in craft stores. Saw the $\frac{3}{8}$" dowel into four 8" lengths for the mallet handles. Saw four 2" pieces from the 1" dowel for the mallet heads.
**2.** Drill a $\frac{1}{2}$" hole part way into each mallet head and hot glue a handle in place. Let it solidify completely before you paint.
**3.** Paint three stripes around each mallet head and around the handle about $\frac{1}{2}$" up from the mallet's head. Then paint a stripe around each ball and paint circles as shown.
**4.** Cut the wire into 5" lengths and bend them into wicket shapes.

# Alice

We were lucky to have been given this unusual piece of eyelet, which features bunnies and mushrooms stitched in pale blue on a white batiste. It's one of those "treasures" that would be difficult to find today, but if you have a sewing machine that does embroidery, this would be a great time to test some of those little embroidery stitches you may not have tried. Many of you probably have bunnies, mushrooms, caterpillars, playing card symbols (at least hearts), and lots of other possibilities right in your very own computerized machine.

*The model is a Götz doll.*

51

# Supplies:

1/2 yd. fabric for yoke dress

3 snaps

2¼ yd. embroidered eyelet edging (6"-wide) for pinafore

2½" Velcro strip

## Yoke Dress

Pattern pieces 75, 76, 77

A yoke dress is a wardrobe standard and can be modified for any number of effects. For instance, you can make the sleeves and skirt any length or use elastic instead of cuffs.

**1.** Cut out two bodice fronts and four bodice backs. Right sides together, sew two back bodices to one front at the shoulder seams. Repeat for the bodice lining.

**2.** Right sides together, pin the bodice lining to the bodice and stitch up one center back, around the neckline, and down the other center back. Clip curves, trim seams, turn right side out, and press. Baste the bodice to its lining around the armholes.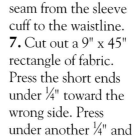

**3.** Cut out two 1½" x 5" cuffs. Gather the sleeve caps between *s. Gather the lower edge of each sleeve.

**4.** Sew the right side of each cuff to the wrong side of each sleeve. Press the remaining long edge of each cuff ¼" toward the wrong side. Fold each cuff to the outside of the sleeve and machine stitch.

**5.** Pull the gathering threads of the sleeve caps to fit the bodice armholes. Pin and stitch.

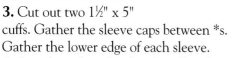

**6.** Sew the underarm seam from the sleeve cuff to the waistline.

**7.** Cut out a 9" x 45" rectangle of fabric. Press the short ends under ¼" toward the wrong side. Press under another ¼" and stitch. To hem, turn the long bottom edge of the skirt under ¼". Turn under another ½" and stitch.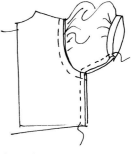

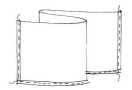

**8.** Gather the top edge of the skirt and sew it to the bodice, right sides together.

**9.** Lapping the right back over the left, sew three snaps evenly spaced to the bodice back.

## Pinafore

Pattern pieces 78, 79

**1.** Cut out a 30" x 5¾" rectangle for the pinafore skirt along the embroidered edge of the 6"-wide eyelet. The waistband is a strip 2" x 12½". Cut out four pinafore bib backs and two fronts. Cut two 1½" x 22½" ruffles so the outer edge of each is placed along the scalloped edging of the eyelet. Cut out two 1¾" x 16" ties.

**2.** Gather the pinafore skirt to fit the waistband. Pin the wrong side of the skirt to the right side of the waistband, with the waistband extending ¼" beyond the skirt. Stitch in place. Press the remaining long edge of the waistband ¼" toward the wrong side. Tucking in the short ends of the waistband, fold the waist-band over to the right side and topstitch all three sides. Set aside.

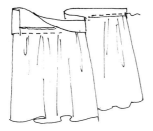

**3.** Sew the pinafore bib front to two backs at the shoulder seams. Repeat for the lining.

**4.** Right sides together, pin the bib to the bib lining, stitching the center backs and around the neckline. Trim the seam allowances, turn right side out, and press.

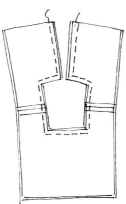

**5.** Because you want the gathered ruffle to be a little wider at the shoulder than at the waistline, you need to give it a little crescent shaping. Trim away about ½" of the width of each end of the ruffles, gradually going back to the original cutting line as you approach the middle of the ruffle.

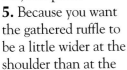

**6.** Gather each ruffle along the curved edge. Pull the gathering threads so the ruffle fits along the entire side of the pinafore bib, waist-band to waistband. Right sides together, stitch in place.

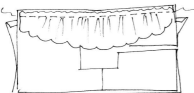

**7.** Press the remaining armhole edge of the pinafore bodice lining ¼" toward the wrong side, enclosing the raw edges. Slipstitch to the ruffle.

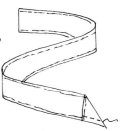

**8.** Narrow hem both long edges of each tie. On one end of each tie, fold the fabric, right sides together, at a 45° angle so the end meets the long edge. Stitch, turn to right side, and press. Make a small pleat in the remaining short end of the tie so it fits on the pinafore waistband. Fold ¼" toward the wrong side and stitch to the waistband where the side seam would be.

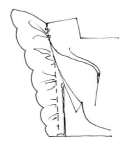

**9.** Pin the bib front to the center front of the pinafore skirt, with the unfinished edge of the bib slightly below the waistband seam. Stitch over the waistband seam to secure the bib. Similarly, sew the pinafore bib backs to the pinafore skirt backs, lining up the center backs.

**10.** Lapping the right over the left ¼", sew Velcro in place at the center backs of the bib.

# Queen of Hearts

This queen's crown is similar to Glinda's, but features sequined heart appliqués. If you can't find this exact type of trim, look for embroidered hearts or make your own from red satin.

*The model is a Götz doll.*

# Supplies:

½ yd. white taffeta
¼ yd. black taffeta
½ yd. red heart flocked netting
2½ yd. gathered red lace (1¼"-wide)
3½ yd. red sequin trim
8 small sequined heart appliqués
1 large sequined heart appliqué
9" elastic (⅛"-wide)
⅛ yd. iridescent satin
⅛ yd. heavyweight clear plastic
3 snaps
2" strip of Velcro
Craft glue stick

# Dress

Pattern pieces 75, 76, 99

**1.** This bodice is self-lined. Cut two bodice fronts and four bodice backs from the black taffeta. Right sides together, sew one front to two backs at the shoulder seams. Repeat for the lining. Place the bodice and its lining right sides together. Stitch around the neck edge and down the center backs.

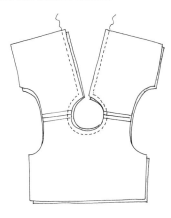

Clip the curves, turn right side out, and press. If you are dealing with particularly slippery fabric, baste the bodice and lining together around all the remaining edges so it's easier to treat it as one unit. Do not sew the side seams until the sleeves are attached.
**2.** Cut two sleeves from white taffeta and two from the red heart netting. Layer the netting sleeves over the right side of the taffeta sleeves and from now on treat the two layers as one.

**3.** To make the elastic casings for the bottom edges of the sleeves, press the lower edges of the sleeves under ¼" and then another ⅜", folding both the taffeta and netting layers at the same time. Stitch along the folded edge to make a casing.
**4.** Cut the elastic in half and thread each piece through a sleeve casing. Anchor the ends with a few stitches.
**5.** Gather the sleeve caps to fit the bodice armholes and stitch them in place, right sides together.

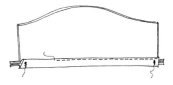

**6.** Sew the underarm seams from the sleeve elastic down to the waistline of the bodice.

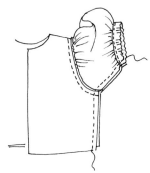

**7.** Cut a 45" x 12" rectangle of white taffeta for the skirt. Cut a 42½" x 9½" rectangle of red netting for the overskirt.
**8.** Hem one long edge of the taffeta skirt by pressing it under ¼" and then 1". Stitch.
**9.** Fold the netting in half crosswise, wrong sides together. Cut along the fold line, then round off the front corners simultaneously by cutting through both layers of netting as indicated.

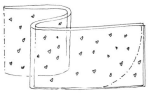

**10.** Apply the red gathered lace to the bottom edges of the netting so the heading of the lace covers about ¼" of the netting. Stitch in place.

**11.** Machine stitch red sequin trim over the previous stitching.

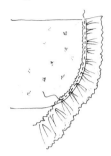

**12.** Pin the top edges of the netting overskirt to the top edge of the taffeta skirt, wrong side of net to right side of taffeta. From now on, treat both layers as one skirt.

**13.** Press the center back edges of the skirt under ¼". Press them under another ¼" and stitch. Gather the top edge of the skirt and fit it to the bodice. Right sides together, sew the skirt to the bodice, center back edges of the skirt even with the finished center back edges of the bodice. Lapping the right over the left by ¼", sew the snaps to the center back edges of the bodice.

**14.** Glue two small sequined heart appliqués to the center of the bodice as shown.

# Crown

Pattern piece 80

**1.** Cut one crown of iridescent satin and one of clear plastic. Layer the two, wrong side of satin to the plastic. Use a glue stick to keep them together.

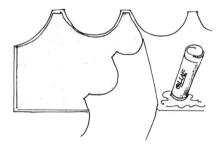

**2.** Glue stick the sequin trim to the satin side of the crown, all around the edges, then topstitch the sequins to the crown.

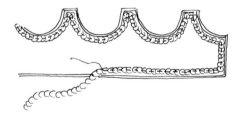

**3.** Try the crown on the doll to measure the overlap you need. Sew Velcro to the back edges of the crown.

**4.** Glue the large sequined heart to the center front of the crown. Glue six small sequined hearts to the points of the crown. (You will probably need a new sewing machine needle after this project.)

# The White Rabbit

Our white rabbit sports a watch pin so he can keep track of the time. Other options are novelty buttons that look like a watch pin, or you could make one out of felt scraps, drawing a face with a fine permanent marker.

*The model is a Creative Doll Company doll.*

57

## Supplies:

¹/₂ yd. white acrylic fur
1 Velcro strip
15" elastic (³/₈"-wide)
12" white bias tape
¹/₄ yd. vest fabric
¹/₄ yd. vest lining fabric
4 buttons (³/₈")
4 Velcro circles or snaps
Cotton ball

## Body

Pattern pieces  81,  82,  83,  84,  85

**1.** Cut out two sides of the rabbit body, four ears, two paws, two arms, and one hood.
**2.** Fold one rabbit body piece in half lengthwise with right sides together. Stitch the shoulder seam. Repeat for the other half of the body.

**3.** Open both body pieces and pin them right sides together. Stitch the back seam.
**4.** Stitch the front seam from the end of the Velcro opening to the crotch.

**5.** Refold the body so the back and front seams line up on top of each other, with right sides together. Stitch the leg seams.

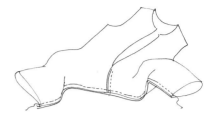

**6.** Pin a round paw to the bottom of each leg with right sides together. Stitch. Clip the curves.

**7.** Fold the arms lengthwise with right sides together. Stitch the arm seams. Clip the curves around the paw.

**8.** Pin the arm opening to the rabbit body. The mid-shoulder seam lines up with the middle of the lengthwise fold of the arm. The arm seam will line up with the base of the armhole. Stitch around the armhole and clip the curves. Repeat with the other arm.

**9.** Complete the hood by sewing the two back seams.

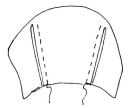

Sew the seam binding to the right side of the hood face opening. Fold it toward the inside of the hood and stitch along the other edge to form a casing. Run 8" of elastic through the binding. Sew the elastic at both ends to secure the elastic in place.

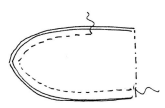

**10.** Run a gathering stitch along the neck edge of the hood. Gather the neck edge of the hood to line up with the neck edge of the body, right sides together. Stitch the neck seam.

**11.** Right sides together, pin each ear to a lining. Stitch. Turn right side out. Stitch across the open end at the bottom of each ear.

**12.** Pin the bottom edge of each ear to the curved line on the hood near the top of the back seams. Hand stitch both ears to the hood, making sure to put in some extra stitches in front to help the ears stand up.

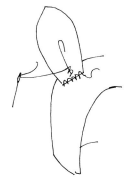

**13.** Cut a 6" strip of Velcro in half lengthwise. Sew to the front opening of the body.

**14.** Sew a white cotton ball on the backside for a tail.

## Bow Tie

**1.** To make a bow tie, cut a scrap of fabric 3" x 4". Fold it in half lengthwise with right sides together and stitch. Turn right side out and stitch across the short ends. Press it so the seam ends up in the center of the bow's back.

**2.** Cut a 1" x 4" strip of tie material to act as the center of the bow. Fold it lengthwise to cover the raw edges and wrap it tightly around the center of the bow tie. Stitch in place. Connect the ends of the tie with 7" of elastic. Slip the tie into place over the doll's head.

# Vest

Pattern piece 86

**1.** Cut one vest and one vest lining.

**2.** Fold the first third of the vest lengthwise with right sides together. Stitch the shoulder seam. Repeat for the other third of the vest.

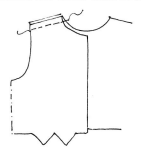

**3.** Repeat for the lining.

**4.** Right sides together, pin the lining to the vest. Stitch the vest to the lining, starting at the bottom of the vest and going around, stopping 2" before you get back to the starting point. Clip the curves, trim the seams, turn right side out, and press. Hand stitch the 2" opening closed.

**5.** To finish the armholes, press the vest and the lining armhole edges ¼" toward the wrong side. Pin the vest armholes to the lining armholes and hand stitch.

**6.** Sew the decorative buttons and Velcro circles or snaps in place on the vest front.

 # The Wizard of Oz

# The Road to the Emerald City Setting

Quilt shops are a wonderful source of unusual fabrics. We actually found a yellow brick patterned print! You can always use plain yellow fabric, even felt, and draw geometric patterns with a marker. As for the Emerald City, we dug through our glittery scraps and found several in the emerald to jade family.

# Supplies:

Cardboard project display board,
   48" x 36"
1⅓ yd. sky blue felt for Land of Oz sky
*Optional:* 1⅔ yd. green felt for foreground and
   grassy hills on background
Scraps of bright floral printed fabrics for poppy
   fields and more-vivid-than-real-life flowers
Scraps of coordinating print fabrics for hills in the
   distance
1 yd. of yellow brick printed fabric for road
Scraps of contrasting felt for hot air balloon
Hot glue gun
Spray adhesive
Craft glue stick

# Setting

Pattern pieces 87, 88, 89

**1.** Using a pencil, draw a rolling horizon line across the front of the display board. Cut the sky blue felt to fit the top part and green felt for the hills. Following the manufacturer's instructions, spray adhesive sparingly over the entire display board. Let it dry a bit before you stretch the sky and hills felts over the board, working out any bubbles with your fingers. Trim away excess felt along the cardboard edges.

**2.** Cut out simple flowery field shapes and use spray adhesive to apply them to the background.

**3.** Cut out the basic Emerald City skyline from green felt. You will make the city as a separate, removable piece. Because it is made of felt, it will stick to the felt background while in use. Cut out the various building segments from several different green glittery fabrics and glue them in place with spray adhesive on the green skyline felt. Add windows or other jewel trims as your imagination dictates.

**4.** Cut out the hot air balloon pieces from felt scraps of your own color choice and either glue them in place with spray adhesive or use the balloon as a removable component of the setting.

**5.** Lay out the green felt and cut a curved road from the yellow brick fabric, extending it up from the foreground into the background. Remember to make it narrower as it gets closer to the Emerald City to account for distance and perspective.

# Scary Forest Setting

This setting is identical to Hansel and Gretel's, except we omitted the gingerbread house and men and the witch's oven. If you are wondering why that pesky mouse appears in this scene as well as Cinderella's, remember that the Cowardly Lion was so timid he was even afraid of a mouse. Also, you could act out the fable about the mouse removing a thorn from the paw of a fierce lion.

## Supplies:

Cardboard project display board, 48" x 36"
1¹⁄₃ yd. deep blue felt for scary forest sky
*Optional:* 1¹⁄₂ yd. green felt for foreground
Scraps of brown and green print fabrics for tree trunks and leaf clusters
Scraps of variegated green fabrics for grass and ground
Gray polymer clay for mouse
2 blue rhinestones or glass-headed pins for mouse's eyes
Spray adhesive
Craft glue stick

## Setting

Pattern pieces 46, 47

**1.** Following the manufacturer's instructions, spray adhesive sparingly over the entire front of the display board. Let it dry a bit before you stretch the felt over the board, working out any bubbles with your fingers. Trim away excess felt along the cardboard edges.
**2.** Cut out simple grass yard shapes and use spray adhesive to apply it to the background. Cut out a tree trunk and leaf clusters and glue the Scary Forest in place.

## Mouse

**1.** Following the manufacturer's instructions, mold a mouse body, head, ears, and tail from gray polymer clay. Insert rhinestone or glass-head pins for eyes, then bake as directed. To

keep it simple (and not reveal our total lack of sculpting skills), this mouse has no limbs, but he sits up nicely anyway.

# Dorothy

For a simple farm girl, Dorothy sure has fancy shoes! In the children's novel she wore emerald slippers, but we prefer ruby. When making them yourself, you can choose.

*The model is a Götz doll.*

## Supplies:

¼ yd. white broadcloth
½ yd. blue/white gingham
1 yd. narrow blue RickRack
9" elastic (⅛"-wide)
2 white buttons (½")
3" Velcro strip
1 hook and eye
Hot glue gun
Small stuffed dog to play the role of Toto
Basket for Toto's transportation
**Ruby Slippers:**
Scrap of red knit metallic fabric
⅓ yd. red sequins-by-the-yard
2 red plastic "jewels" (⅜")

## Blouse

Pattern pieces 15, 16, 17

**1.** Cut one front and two backs from the white broadcloth. Right sides together, sew the shoulder seams.
**2.** Press the center back edges under ⅛" twice and stitch.
**3.** Cut a 1" x 8¾" bias strip of white fabric. Pin it to the neckline of the blouse so one long edge is flush with the neckline and the short ends extend ¼" beyond the center backs. Stitch in place.
**4.** Grade seam allowances. Tucking in the short ends, fold the bias over twice and slipstitch. Sew RickRack over the stitching line.

**5.** Zigzag or serge the bottom edge of the sleeves, then turn under and stitch by machine (or use your rolled hem attachment).

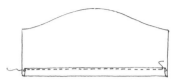

**6.** Fold the bottom of each sleeve under another ⅜" and stitch to form a casing. Sew RickRack over the casing's stitching line.

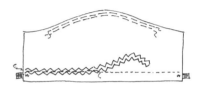

**7.** Gather the caps of the sleeves between *s on the pattern piece.

Right sides together, stitch the sleeves to the blouse armholes. Cut the elastic in half and thread each piece through a sleeve casing. Anchor with a few stitches.
**8.** Right sides together, sew the underarm seams from the sleeve elastic to the waistline.

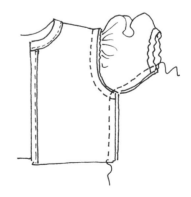

**9.** Hem the bottom edge of the blouse by pressing it under ¼" twice and stitching.
**10.** Sew the Velcro strip to the blouse center backs, lapping the right over the left by about ¼".

## Jumper

**1.** Cut a 8½" x 45" rectangle of the gingham fabric for the skirt. Cut a 1¾" x 12¾" waistband. Cut a 2" x 6" bib. Cut two 1½" x 9½" straps.
**2.** Hem the short sides (center backs) and one long edge of the jumper skirt by pressing them under ¼" twice and stitching.
**3.** Fold the waistband lengthwise, right sides together. Stitch the short ends. Turn right side out and press.
**4.** Gather the remaining edge of the skirt to fit the waistband. Right sides together, sew the skirt to the waistband.

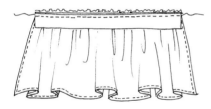

**5.** Wrong sides together, fold the bib in half so it measures 2" x 3". Press each long edge of each strap ¼" toward the wrong side, then fold it in half lengthwise, wrong sides together. Enclose the 3" long sides of the bib ¼" inside the folded

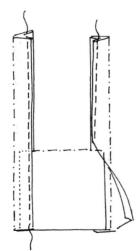

straps and flush with one end. Stitch along the edge the whole length of the straps.
**6.** Center the bib on the wrong side of the waistband and stitch over the previous waistband-to-skirt stitching. Finish the seam allowance.

**7.** Sew the hook and eye at the back waistband opening, lapping the right over the left. Sew buttons on the waistband front just over the straps.

## Ruby Slippers

Pattern pieces 112, 113

**1.** Cut out four shoe uppers and two soles from the red metallic fabric. These are self-lined shoes.
**2.** Pin one upper to a lining, right sides together. Stitch around the inside curved edge. Clip the curves, trim the seams, and open out. Press carefully (this type of material is sensitive to hot irons).

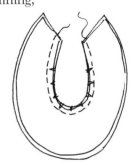

**3.** Right sides together, sew the heel seam. Fold the lining down and treat both layers of fabric as one from now on.
**4.** Pin the sole of the shoe to the upper. Straight stitch, then use a narrow zigzag to prevent raveling. Turn right side out.
**5.** Hand stitch the sequin trim around each shoe. Cut two strips of the red metallic fabric 1" x 3". Fold the strips wrong sides together lengthwise and gather along the raw edges. Pull the gathering thread to make a ruffled circle or rosette. Tucking the finished ends under, stitch the rosette to the slipper front. Hot glue a gem to the middle of each rosette.

# Wicked Witch

Every good adventure needs a villain, and in the Wizard of Oz, the Wicked Witch fills the bill perfectly.

*The model is a Faithful Friends by Heidi Ott doll.*

## Supplies:

1 yd. black fabric
13" black grosgrain ribbon ($^1/_4$"-wide)
32" black bias tape
Scrap of heavy interfacing
3 snaps
Velcro dot
8" dowel, $^3/_8$"-diameter for broomstick
Children's watercolor paints and brush
Raffia scraps for broom

## Blouse

Pattern pieces 90, 91, 92, 93

**1.** Cut out two fronts, four backs, two upper sleeves, and two lower sleeves. This blouse is self-lined.
**2.** Right sides together, sew one front to two backs at the shoulder seams. Repeat for lining.
**3.** Pin the blouse to its lining, right sides together, and sew up one center back, around the neckline and down the other center back.

Clip the curves, trim the seams, and turn right side out. Press. Baste the lining to the blouse by stitching around the armholes.
**4.** Press the lower edges of the lower sleeves under $^1/_4$" and topstitch.
**5.** Gather the sleeve caps and bottom edges of the upper sleeves. Pull the gathering threads along the bottom edges to fit the top of the lower sleeves. Stitch.

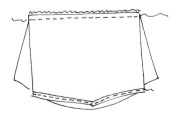

Right sides together, pin the sleeve caps to the blouse armholes, adjusting the gathers to fit, and stitch.
**6.** Right sides together, sew the underarm seams from the wrist to the waist.

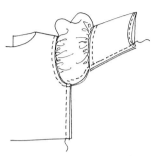

**7.** Zigzag the lower edges of the blouse to prevent raveling.

## Skirt

**1.** Cut a 10" x 25" rectangle of fabric. Press one long edge under $^1/_4$", then press it under another $^1/_4$" and topstitch.
**2.** Hem the center backs (the two short ends of the rectangle) by pressing them under $^1/_4$" twice and topstitching.
**3.** Gather the remaining long edge of the skirt. Make a $^1/_4$" hem in both ends of the grosgrain ribbon and fit the gathered skirt to the ribbon, which will be the waistband. The ribbon should be pinned to the right side of the skirt. Stitch over the gathering line.

**4.** Lapping the right over the left, sew a Velcro dot to the waistband at the center backs.

# Hat

Pattern pieces 94, 95

**1.** Cut one hat crown (pattern piece #94) from interfacing and one from the fabric. Pin the interfacing piece to the wrong side of the fabric piece and baste the straight edges together.

**2.** Treating it as one unit, right sides of fabric together, sew the side seam of the cone. Turn right side out.

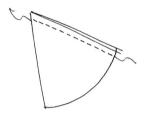

**3.** Cut two brims from the fabric. Right sides together, sew around the outside circle. Turn right side out and press.

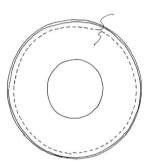

**4.** Stitch the inner brim edges to the cone part of the hat.

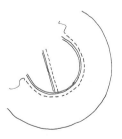

# Cape

Pattern piece 96

**1.** Cut out two cape pieces. Right sides together, sew both sides and the lower edge. Turn right side out.

**2.** Gather both layers of the cape together along the top edge. Pull the gathering threads so the top edge measures 8".

**3.** Center the gathered cape along one edge of the bias tape so 12" of bias tape extends on each side of the cape. Fold the bias tape around the top edge of the cape, enclosing the gathering. Tuck the short ends of the bias tape in. Stitch along the bias tape from one end to the other, enclosing the top edge of the cape in the stitching.

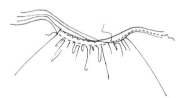

# Wicked Witch's Broom

**1.** Use children's watercolor paint to stain the broomstick brown. Rubber band a small handful of raffia to the bottom of it and wrap the rubber band with more raffia.

# Glinda

For every evil character, there must be a good one who helps the heroine. Glinda sparkles in the role.

The model is a Creative Doll Company doll.

# Supplies:

1 yd. iridescent fabric with lots of body
1 yd. taffeta
1 yd. silver sequin trim
2 yd. pink sequin trim
6 silver star appliqués (1")
1 sequin-covered bow appliqué (or whatever
   shape you can find)
Scrap of silver sequin-like fabric, 7" x 5"
Scrap of heavy interfacing, 7" x 5"
9" elastic ($1/8$"-wide)
5" Velcro strip
25-30 silver plastic glue-on star jewels (14mm)
Heavyweight clear plastic, 4" x 14"
10" dowel, $1/16$"-diameter
Silver glitter paint
Glue stick
Tacky glue

# Dress

Pattern pieces 25, 97, 98, 99

**1.** Cut one front bodice and two back bodices from the iridescent fabric and the taffeta. The taffeta will be the lining. Stitch the front to the backs at the shoulder seams, right sides together. Repeat for the lining.
**2.** Place the bodice and its lining right sides together. Stitch around the neck edge and down the center backs. Clip the curves, turn right side out, and press. If you are dealing with particularly slippery fabric, baste the bodice and lining together around all the remaining edges so it's easier to treat as one unit. Don't sew the side seams until the sleeves are attached.

**3.** Cut two sleeves from the iridescent fabric. Zigzag or serge the bottom edge of the hem, then turn it up $1/4$" and stitch by machine (or use your rolled hem attachment).
**4.** Fold the bottom edge of the sleeve up another $3/8$" and stitch to form a casing. Cut the elastic in half and thread each piece through a sleeve casing. Anchor the ends of the elastic with a few stitches.

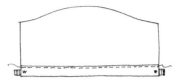

**5.** Gather the sleeve caps to fit the bodice armholes. Right sides together, sew the sleeves to the bodice. Sew the underarm seams from the sleeve elastic to the waistline.

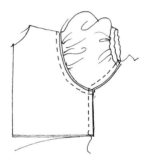

**6.** Cut a 12" x 67" rectangle from both the taffeta and iridescent fabric (this will have to be pieced on the side). Fold each in half and place the basque skirt cutting guide along the top edge and cut out. This creates the area for the pointed front of the bodice to fit.

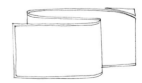

**7.** Hem the short edges and one long edge of the taffeta and iridescent fabric skirts by turning the fabric under $1/4$". Press under another $1/4$" and stitch.
**8.** Right sides up, place the iridescent fabric on top of the taffeta. Gather as one unit across the remaining long edge with the basque waist cutout. Matching the center front point of the

bodice to the center front cutout on the skirt, right sides together, sew the bodice to the skirt.

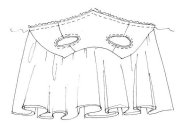

**9.** Stitch silver sequin trim along the waist seam.

**10.** Sew a 3" Velcro strip to the center backs of the bodice, lapping the right over the left about ¼".

**11.** Glue plastic stars to the front of the skirt in a random pattern.

## Crown

Pattern piece 100

**1.** Cut one crown of iridescent fabric and one of clear plastic. Layer the two, wrong side of fabric to the plastic. Use a glue stick to keep them together.

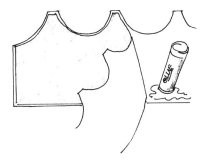

**2.** Glue stick the sequin trim to the satin side of the crown, all around the edges, then topstitch the sequins to the crown.

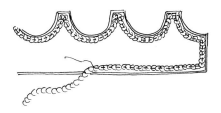

**3.** Try the crown on the doll to measure the overlap you need. Sew 2" of Velcro to the back edges of the crown.

**4.** Glue small stars to each point of the crown with tacky glue.

**5.** Cut two stars of heavy interfacing and two of scrap silver fabric. Use a glue stick to adhere the wrong side of the silver fabric star to the interfacing star. Use tacky glue around the edge of the star to attach the sequin trim. Make a second star for the magic wand.

**6.** Glue one big star to the center front of the crown as shown. (You probably will need a new sewing machine needle after this project.)

## Magic Wand

**1.** Paint the dowel with silver and glitter paint. Hot glue the remaining large star (see step 5 above) on one end of the dowel.

# Scarecrow

To make this character more like a real scarecrow, stuff raffia into the costume so it sticks out the sleeves and pant legs.

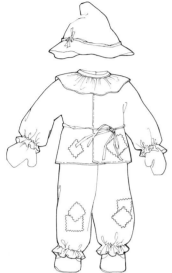

The model is a Götz doll.

## Supplies:

1/4 yd. print fabric for shirt
1/3 yd. pants fabric
1/4 yd. cream broadcloth
1/4 yd. black felt for hat
1 package raffia
2/3 yd. elastic (1/8"-wide)
11 1/2" elastic (1/4"-wide)
2 snaps

## Shirt

Pattern pieces 101, 102

**1.** Cut out two fronts and one back. Right sides together, sew the fronts to the back at the shoulder seams.
**2.** Press the neckline and center front edges 1/4" toward the wrong side. Stitch.
**3.** Zigzag or serge the bottom edge of each sleeve, then turn it up and stitch by machine (or use your rolled hem attachment for a nice hem).
**4.** Cut two pieces of 1/8" elastic 3 1/4" long. Using a pencil, draw a line on the wrong side of the sleeve 1/2" above and parallel to the hemmed sleeve bottom. Using two or three straight stitches, anchor one end of the elastic to the fabric on the line. Switch to a wide enough zigzag stitch to swing back and forth over the elastic, creating a mini-casing. Stretch the elastic as you proceed to the end of the line; straight stitch the elastic to the fabric to anchor it at the end.

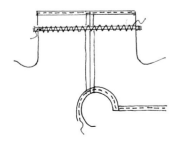

**5.** Sew the underarm seam, starting at the bottom of the sleeve and ending at the lower edge of the shirt.
**6.** Hem the bottom of the shirt by turning it under 1/4" twice and stitching. Sew one snap to the neckline, lapping the left over the right by about 1/4".

## Collar

**1.** Cut a 2" x 16" strip of cream fabric. Cut a 1 1/4" x 8" bias strip.
**2.** Narrow hem one long edge and the short ends of the 16" strip. Gather the remaining long edge.
**3.** Pin the gathered edge to the bias strip so the bias extends beyond the collar by 1/4" on each end. Stitch. Press the remaining long edge under 1/4" toward the wrong side. Tuck in the short ends and fold the collar over the bias so the seam is enclosed. Stitch.
**4.** Sew a snap to the center back.

## Pants

Pattern piece 103

**1.** Cut out two from the pattern. Right sides together, sew the center front and center back seams.
**2.** Narrow hem the bottoms of the pant legs. Zigzag a 4 1/2" piece of elastic to each pant leg just like you did with the shirt sleeves, 1/2" above the hemmed edge.

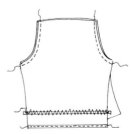

**3.** Zigzag around the waistline edge of the pants. Fold the waist edge over ½" and straight stitch, leaving a 1" opening at the center back to insert elastic.

**4.** Thread the ¼" elastic through the waistline casing and stitch the ends together. Sew the opening closed.

**5.** Sew the inner leg seam.

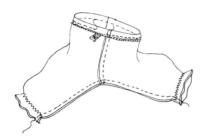

**6.** Cut out patches of various sizes and glue or fuse with fusible web to the pants and shirt. Tie a 20" strand of raffia around the scarecrow's waist

## Hat

Pattern pieces  69,  104

**1.** Cut out one crown and one brim from the felt. Sew the back seam of the crown and trim the seam allowances.

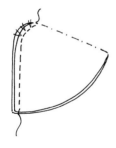

**2.** Right sides together, sew the brim to the crown. Topstitch over the seam. Glue approximately 20" of raffia to the hat and tie a knot on one side.

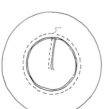

## Mittens

Pattern piece  105

**1.** Cut out four mittens. Press the top edge of each mitten piece  ¼" toward the wrong side. Stitch.

**2.** Right sides together, sew the front and back mitten pieces together, stitching around all sides except the wrist.

**3.** Cut a 3" piece of ⅛" elastic for each mitten and zigzag it to the inside edge of each mitten, ¼" in from the hemmed edge.

## Testimonial

**1.** A testimonial is simply a piece of paper that verifies what a wonderful person you are. Simply roll up a small piece of paper and tie it with a scrap of ribbon.

# Tin Man

W̶ho could forget the Tin Man who really had the biggest heart of all? He must keep his funnel handy at all times, so he wears it on his head.

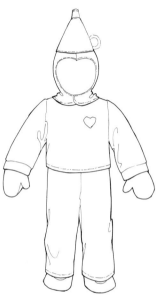

*The model is a Götz doll.*

## Supplies:

1 yd. metallic-look knit fabric
Scrap of heavy interfacing
11½" elastic (¼"-wide) for pants
6" elastic (⅛"-wide) for mittens
4 snaps
1 gray pipe cleaner
1 red plastic faceted sew-on heart, ½" - ¾" tall

## Shirt

### Pattern pieces 106, 107, 108

**1.** Cut out one front, two backs, and two sleeves from the metallic-look knit fabric. At this point it would be a good idea to make sure you have a brand new machine needle installed, because this type of fabric can catch on a rough needle. Right sides together, sew the front to the backs at the shoulder seams.
**2.** Zigzag or serge around the neckline and the center back edges. Fold them ¼" toward the wrong side and topstitch.
**3.** Zigzag or serge the lower edges of the sleeves, fold them under ¼" and topstitch.

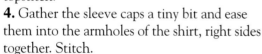

**4.** Gather the sleeve caps a tiny bit and ease them into the armholes of the shirt, right sides together. Stitch.
**5.** Starting at the wrist, sew the underarm seams all the way to the waist. To hem the bottom edge of the shirt, zigzag or serge it, then fold it under ¼" and stitch.
**6.** Lapping the right center back over the left, sew three snaps.
**7.** Sew the heart in the appropriate place on the front of the shirt.

## Pants

### Pattern piece 109

**1.** Cut out two pants pieces. Right sides together, zigzag or serge the center back and center front seams.
**2.** Zigzag or serge the bottom of the pant legs. Fold them under ¼" and topstitch.
**3.** Zigzag or serge the inner leg seam.

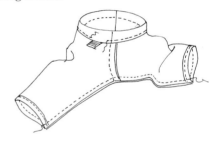

**4.** Zigzag around the waistline edge to prevent raveling. To form a casing, fold the finished edge ½" toward the inside of the garment and straight stitch, leaving a 1" opening at the center back to insert the elastic.
**5.** Thread the elastic through the casing and stitch the ends together. Hand stitch the opening closed.

## Hood

### Pattern piece 110

**1.** Cut out two hoods. Sew the dart at the top of each piece. Right sides together, sew the two pieces together, starting at the top of the face opening and continuing as shown. The two darts should line up.

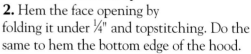

**2.** Hem the face opening by folding it under ¼" and topstitching. Do the same to hem the bottom edge of the hood.
**3.** Sew a snap to the neckline of the hood as indicated on the pattern piece.

# Funnel

### Pattern piece 111

**1.** Cut one from metallic fabric and one from interfacing, using appropriate cutting lines for each. Fold the curved edges of the fabric around the interfacing and stitch along the top and bottom.

**2.** Right sides together, sew the back seam through both layers.

**3.** Cut a 1½" x 2" piece of fabric and a 1" x 2" piece of interfacing. Fold one 2" edge of the fabric around the interfacing and stitch. Together, the layered piece now measures 1" x 2".

**4.** Roll the layered piece so you have a 1" long tube. Overlapping the edges so the tube fits through the opening in the funnel, push it up into the funnel. Slipstitch the overlapping edges closed. Slipstitch the tube into the funnel opening so only ¾" of the tube remains inside the funnel.

**5.** Cut the pipe cleaner in half and twist the two parts together. Form it into a circle and tack the ends to the funnel to make the handle.

**6.** Put the hood on the doll and set the funnel on top as shown in the photograph. Tack the funnel edge to the hood.

# Shoes

### Pattern pieces 112, 113

**1.** Cut out four shoe uppers and two soles from the metallic fabric. These are self-lined shoes.

**2.** Pin one upper to a lining, right sides together. Stitch around the inside curved edge. Clip the curves, trim the seams, and open out. Press carefully (this type of material is sensitive to hot irons).

**3.** Right sides together, sew the heel seam. Fold the lining down and treat both layers of fabric as one from now on.

**4.** Pin the sole of the shoe to the upper. Straight stitch, then use a narrow zigzag to prevent raveling. Turn right side out.

# Mittens

### Pattern piece 105

**1.** Cut four from fabric. Pin two halves together for each mitten, right sides together. Stitch along the outside edge, leaving the straight edge open to turn.

**2.** Clip the curves and turn right side out. Fold the wrist edge under ¼" and stitch.

**3.** Cut the ⅛"-wide elastic in half and zigzag each half to a mitten, just inside the stitched edge. Overlap the ends of the elastic.

# Cowardly Lion

E̲ven though we are very brave, sometimes we need a medal to prove it to the world.

The model is a Faithful Friends by Heidi Ott doll.

## Supplies:

¹/₂ yd. thick polyester fleece
¹/₄ yd. fun fur with long nap
12" bias tape
8" elastic (¹/₄"-wide)
6" Velcro strip
1 pipe cleaner or wire
Scraps of fiberfill
1 pin back, ³/₄" long
Scrap of ⁷/₈"-wide striped ribbon
Scrap of light cardboard
Tiny scrap of felt for medal
Craft glue stick

## Body

Pattern pieces  81,  83,  84,  85,  114

**1.** Cut out two sides of the lion body, four ears, two paws, and two arms from the fleece. Cut out one hood from the fur.
**2.** Fold one lion body piece in half lengthwise with right sides together. Stitch the shoulder seam. Repeat for the other half of the body.

**3.** Open both body pieces and pin them right sides together. Stitch the back seam.
**4.** Stitch the front seam from the end of the Velcro opening to the crotch.

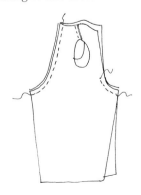

**5.** Refold the body so the back and front seams line up on top of each other, with right sides together. Stitch the leg seams.

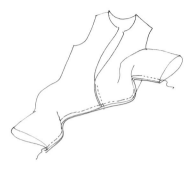

**6.** Pin a round paw to the bottom of each leg with right sides together. Stitch. Clip the curves.

**7.** Fold the arms lengthwise with right sides together. Stitch the arm seams. Clip the curves around the paw.

**8.** Pin the arm opening to the lion body. The mid-shoulder seam lines up with the middle of the lengthwise fold of the arm. The arm seam lines up with the base of the armhole. Stitch around the armhole and clip the curves. Repeat with the other arm.

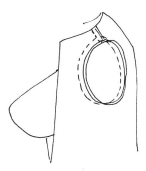

**9.** Complete the hood by sewing the two back seams.

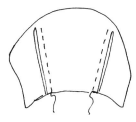

Stitch both sides of the seam binding along the front edge of the hood. Run 8" of elastic through the binding. Sew the elastic at both ends to secure the elastic in place.

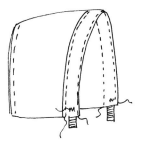

**10.** Run a gathering stitch along the neck edge of the hood. Gather the hood and stitch the neck edge to the neckline of the body suit so the body extends ½" beyond the hood on each center front.

**11.** Right sides together, sew the ear fronts to the backs. Clip the curves and turn right side out.

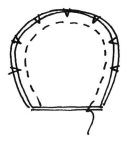

**12.** Make a ½" fold in the center of the bottom edge of each ear and stitch. Hand stitch the ears to the hood where marked on the pattern piece.

**13.** Cut the strip of Velcro in half. Fold the right center front edge of the suit ¼" toward the wrong side and sew the loop side under it. Sew the hook side to the left center front.

**14.** Cut a 3" x 11" piece of the fleece and a 1½" x 5" piece of the fur. Fold the fleece lengthwise, right sides together. Sew the one long seam and one short end to make the tail. Turn right side out.

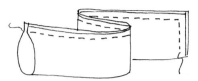

Place a pipe cleaner or wire inside so you can pose the tail later. Cut off any excess wire. Stuff the tail lightly with fiberfill.

**15.** Wrap the stitched end of the tail with the fur piece. Fold one short end under and stitch it to the end of the tail. Also stitch the long fur edge to the tail.

**16.** Fold the unstitched end of the tail ¼" toward the wrong side. Stitch to the back seam of the body suit.

# Medal

Pattern pieces 115, 116

**1.** Cut a piece of light cardboard in the shape of the medal. Cut the striped ribbon in the same shape and glue the ribbon to the cardboard.

**2.** Cut a small circle of felt for the actual hanging medal. Trace the cross pattern onto a scrap of metallic fabric. Cut out the metallic cross and glue it to the felt circle. Or purchase a shiny metal button for the hanging medal.

**3.** Glue the felt circle to the point of the ribbon.

**4.** Glue the medal to the pin back.

# Goldilocks & the Three Bears

# Baby Bear's Bedroom Set

Who needs fine wood furniture for your doll? In the theater, where all is make-believe, we use foam board, a utility knife, and hot glue.

## Supplies:

Cardboard project display board, 48" x 36"
1½ yd. pastel fabric for "wallpaper"
2 sheets white foam board, 20" x 30" x ⅜"
Pkg. wood-grained adhesive vinyl
¾ yd. fabric for mattress
Fiberfill to stuff mattress and pillow
1 yd. fabric for matching quilt top and curtains
⅔ yd. fabric for quilt backing, pillow, and table-cloth
Thin batting for quilt, 18" x 18½"
30" dowel, ⅜"-diameter
2 packages of polymer clay to make porridge bowls
Hot glue gun
Spray adhesive
Craft glue stick
Utility knife

*Note:* For the furniture sewing, use ½" seam allowances to make them more durable.

## Setting

**1.** Cut a 20"-wide x 12"-high window out of the display board 19" up from the floor.
**2.** Cut the "wallpaper" fabric so it fits the display board plus about 2" around all edges. Following the manufacturer's instructions, spray adhesive sparingly over the entire front of the display board. Let it dry a bit before you attempt to lay the fabric out on it because if it is too wet, it can spot the fabric. Stretch the fabric out over the board, working out any bubbles with your fingers. You can usually lift the fabric up and reposition it if necessary. Remember to cut out the fabric that covers the window and fold and glue the raw edges out to the back side of the board. Using a glue stick, secure the raw edges of the fabric to the back side of the board.
**3.** Cut a slit in each fold of the display board and the fabric about 1" long and approximately 1" above the top of the window. Insert the dowel into the slits from the front of the covered display board, hanging the curtains before the second end is inserted.

**4.** We used 1½ yd. of tan felt for the floor in this scene, but there's no need for a special fabric. Children will use whatever is available in their rooms for carpet or flooring.

## Bed

**1.** Cut two 12" x 22½" pieces of foam board for the top and bottom of the bed frame. Cut two 4½" x 22½" pieces for the sides of the bed frame. Cut two 4½" x 11½" pieces for the ends of the bed frame.
**2.** Cut a 12" x 11" headboard and a 12" x 7" foot board.
**3.** Using the glue gun, glue the corners of the bed frame as shown.

**4.** Quickly apply glue to one side of the frame along the narrow edges of the foam board and attach the bed bottom piece. When cool, apply glue to the other side of the frame along the edges and attach the bed top piece. You now have a closed box.

**5.** Use adhesive vinyl to cover the parts of the foot board and headboard that will show after they are attached to the bed. We found it works best to wrap the surfaces that face the camera in the photo, leaving about ½" extra adhesive paper going around to the other side. Then cut a piece of vinyl slightly smaller than the other side of each piece and center it on the less visible surface. Don't cover the part of the foam board that will be glued to the bed frame because the glue adheres better to the foam board than the vinyl covering.

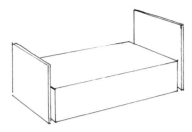

**6.** Hot glue the foot board and headboard in place.

**7.** Cover the top, bottom, and sides of the box you have formed with wood-grained adhesive paper.

**8.** After you have finished making the quilt and curtains, cut motifs from leftovers of that fabric and glue stick them to the headboard and foot board.

## Mattress

**1.** Cut two 14½" x 25" pieces of mattress fabric. Right sides together, sew around all four sides, leaving a 5" opening at one short end for turning and stuffing.

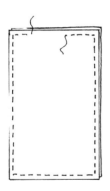

**2.** Turn the mattress right side out, press, and stuff with fiberfill to the desired firmness. Hand stitch the opening closed.

## Pillow

**1.** Cut two 6" x 9" rectangles of pillow fabric. Right sides together, sew around three sides, leaving one short end open. Turn right side out, press, and stuff with fiberfill.

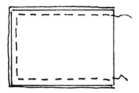

**2.** Tuck the raw edges of the opening ½" into the pillow and machine stitch across the open end.

## Quilt

**1.** Cut out a quilt top 18" wide x 17½" long. Cut out a quilt backing 19½" wide x 19" long. Cut out two 1¾" x 19½" border strips and two 1¾" x 17½" border strips.

**2.** Right sides together, sew the 17½" border strips to the 17½" sides of the quilt top. Sew the 19½" long border strips to the top and bottom sides of the quilt top. Press. The completed quilt top should measure 19½" wide x 19" long.

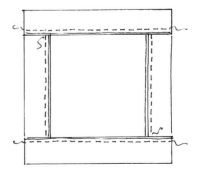

**3.** Make a "quilt sandwich," layering from the bottom up, first the batting, then the quilt top right side up, then the backing right side down. Stitch around all four sides, leaving a 5" opening to turn. Turn right side out, press, and hand stitch the opening closed.

## Table

**1.** Cut four 4" x 6½" pieces of foam board for the sides of the table. Cut a circle approximately 7" in diameter by tracing around a small plate or other circular object, or cut a 7" square for the tabletop.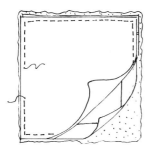

**2.** Hot glue the corners of the table together so you have a square pedestal 6½" tall. Cover all four sides with wood-grained adhesive vinyl.

**3.** Apply hot glue to the top edges of the pedestal and place the tabletop on top.

## Tablecloth

**1.** Cut out a circle of fabric, using a larger circular object than the tabletop. If you made a square tabletop, cut out a square of fabric. Press the raw edge under about ½" and machine hem.

## Porridge Bowls

**1.** Following the manufacturer's instructions, mold three bowls from polymer clay, using your favorite colors, and bake.

## Curtains

**1.** Cut out two curtains, each 13" wide x 18" long. These curtains are just props, so there's no need to hem each edge twice. Hem the long edges by pressing them under ¼" and stitching. Press the shorter edges under 1" and stitch, forming a casing at the top.

**2.** The print fabric we chose had cute little motifs that were perfect for cutting out and gluing to the wall of the setting. They look like family portraits. Another trick is to cut out small pictures from magazines and catalogs and frame them with poster board or fabric frames.

# Goldilocks

We pictured Goldilocks as a brave, curious, and adventuresome child. She also was somewhat spoiled, so we gave her a fancy heirloom pinafore with a scalloped hem, French lace, and embroidered bullion roses. If you cannot locate entredeux or fine cotton laces in your local fabric store, just use the nicest lace you can find and zigzag it directly to the fabric. To simplify the embroidery, you could use lazy daisies, machine embroidery, or even fabric paint.

*The model is a Faithful Friends by Heidi Ott doll.*

## Supplies:

1/2 yd. fabric for yoke dress
9" elastic (1/8"-wide)
3 snaps
1/2 yd. good quality batiste for pinafore
4 yd. flat cotton lace (1"-wide)
2 1/3 yd. entredeux
Pink and green embroidery floss
3 snaps

## Yoke Dress

Pattern pieces 75, 76, 77

**1.** Cut out two bodice fronts, four bodice backs, and two sleeves. Right sides together, sew the two back bodices to one front at the shoulder seams. Repeat for the bodice lining.

**2.** Right sides together, pin the bodice lining to the bodice and stitch up one center back, around the neckline, and down the other center back. Clip the curves, trim the seams, turn right side out, and press. Baste the bodice to its lining around the armholes.

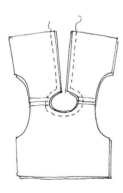

**3.** Zigzag or serge the lower edge of each sleeve, then turn them under and machine stitch (or use your machine's rolled hem attachment).

**4.** Cut the elastic in half. Using a pencil, draw a line on the wrong side of the sleeve 3/4" above and parallel to the hemmed sleeve bottom. Using two or three straight stitches, anchor one end of the elastic to the fabric on the line. Switch to a wide enough zigzag stitch to swing back and forth over the elastic, creating a mini-casing. Stretch the elastic as you proceed to the end of the line; straight stitch

the elastic to the fabric to anchor it at the end.

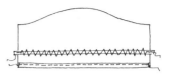

**5.** Gather the sleeve caps between *s on the pattern piece. Right sides together, stitch each sleeve to a bodice armhole.

**6.** Sew the underarm seam from the sleeve to the waistline.

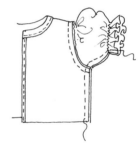

**7.** For the skirt, cut out a 9" x 45" rectangle of fabric. Press the short ends under 1/4" toward the wrong side. Press under another 1/4" and stitch. To hem, turn the long bottom edge of the skirt under 1/4". Turn under another 1/2" and stitch.

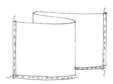

**8.** Gather the top edge of the skirt and sew it to the bodice, right sides together.

**9.** Lapping right back over left, sew three snaps evenly spaced to the bodice back.

# Scalloped Pinafore

Pattern pieces 117, 118

**1.** Place the pinafore bib front pattern piece under a double layer of the bastiste and trace with a pencil or washout marker, but don't cut the two bib fronts out yet.

**2.** For the pinafore skirt, draw a 6¼" x 40" rectangle on the batiste, but don't cut it out yet. Using pattern piece #118, trace the scallop 10 times along one long side of the rectangle. Trace the bullion rosebud in each scallop and the nosegay of bullion rosebuds on one of the bib fronts.

**3.** Using a small embroidery hoop, a #7 or 8 embroidery needle, and two strands of floss, work the flowers as shown.

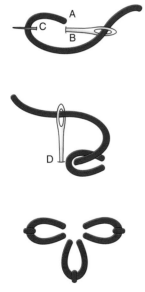

Lazy Daisy Stitch
Come up at A and form a loop. Go down at B (as close to A as possible, but not into it) and come up at C, bringing the needle tip over the thread. Go down at D, making a small anchor stitch.

Bullion Knot
Bring the needle through the fabric, then insert it a short distance away, letting the point emerge at the same place as the thread. Coil the thread around the needle six or seven times, then pull the needle through the coil. Hold the coil down on the fabric with your left thumb. Pull the working thread in the opposite direction to make the coil lie flat, then insert the needle in the same place as before.

When all embroidery is finished, press it right side down on a clean towel, then cut out the bibs and pinafore skirt along the traced lines.

**4.** Right sides together, sew the bib to the bib lining across the scalloped top only, leaving the sides and bottom unstitched. Clip the curves and trim the seam allowances. Turn right side out and press.

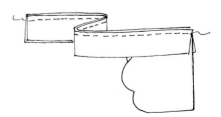

**5.** Cut out four 2½" x 11" straps. Sew a strap to each side of the bib front by sandwiching the bib between two straps as shown. Stitch along the bib side of one long edge of the straps. Turn the straps right side out and press.

**6.** Cut two pieces of entredeux the same length as the straps. Trim away almost all of the excess fabric on one side of the entredeux. Treating both layers of the strap as one unit, and right sides together, zigzag the entredeux to the unfinished side of each strap, keeping the strap exposed ⅛" beyond the entredeux. This extension will curl right into the zigzagging and make a clean finish.

**7.** Cut two pieces of lace, each double the length of the straps. Pull the gathering thread so the lace fits the strap. With right sides up and the entredeux flush with the lace heading, zigzag the lace to the entredeux.

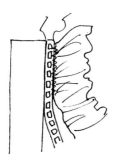

**8.** Trim away most of the excess fabric from one edge of the remaining entredeux. Right sides together, pin the entredeux to the pinafore skirt along the scallops, mitering

the corners. Zigzag the entredeux in place and press. Pull the gathering thread of the remaining lace and spread it out evenly along the scallops. Right sides up, zigzag the lace to the entredeux.

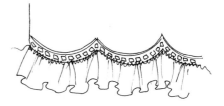

**9.** Narrow hem the center backs (short ends of the rectangle) of the pinafore skirt. Run a gathering thread along the top of the pinafore skirt. Cut out a 1½" x 11" waistband on grain. With the right side of the waistband to the wrong side of the pinafore skirt and the ends of the waistband extending ¼" beyond the center backs of the skirt, sew the waistband to the pinafore. Press the remaining long edge of the waistband ¼" toward the wrong side. Tucking in the ends, fold the waistband to the outside of the garment and topstitch in place.

**10.** Center the bib on the pinafore skirt with the bottom of the bib extending approximately ¼" beyond the bottom edge of the waistband and topstitch it in place.

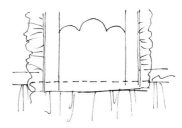

**11.** Try the pinafore on the doll and mark where the waistband snap should go, lapping the right back over the left. Cross the straps in back and mark where you want the snaps on the straps. The snaps should be 1" on either side of the center back.

# About the Authors

Joan Hinds (aka Little Red Riding Hood) and Jean Becker (aka Granny) have been designing patterns together for ten years. What started out as a home-based business soon developed into a small publishing company called Fancywork and Fashion. Together, Joan and Jean have collaborated on eight pattern books, including the *Best Doll Clothes Book* and *Sew the Essential Wardrobe for 18-Inch Dolls*. They live and work in Duluth, Minnesota.

Oh, the wolf? He's their agent.

## Adventures With Polarfleece

*A Sewing Expedition*

by Nancy Cornwell

Nancy Cornwell will lead you on a sewing expedition. Explore and discover endless project possibilities for the entire family. Sew a collection of 15 projects for play, work, fashion, comfort and warmth. The heart of a fallen-away sewer will soon be recaptured and new sewers will be intrigued and inspired.

Softcover • 8-1/2 x 11 • 160 pages
200 color photos • 150 color illustrations
**AWPF • $19.95**

## The Crafter's Guide to Glues

by Tammy Young

Finally, a book that sorts out the bewildering array of glues, adhesives and fusible webs. Choose the right glues for every task and learn how to bond materials and surfaces of any sort. Chapter projects offer practice solving the stickiest of problems.

Softcover • 8-1/4 x 10-7/8 • 96 pages
4-page color section
**CGTG • $14.95**

## Bean Bag Toys: Fashion, Furniture, and Fun!

by Kathryn Severns

Looking for something fun to do with your bean bag toys? Why not dress them up and play with them! Included are 16 adorable outfits, each with full-size patterns and simple, straight-forward instructions, so you can dress up your toys like a witch, cheerleader, barbecue chef, or pirate. In addition to clever outfits, furniture, and accessories, you are treated to party ideas from decorations, activities, and games to delicious recipes that will appeal to children of all ages.

Softcover • 8-1/4 x 10-7/8
112 pages • 90 color photos
**BBFF • $19.95**

## Warman's Dolls

by R. Lane Herron

For both doll collectors and dealers, this is the most complete and useful guide available which covers dolls dating from 1822 to the late 1950s. All of the most collectible lines, for example, Bru, Jumeau, and Lenci are included. In keeping with the Warman's tradition of high quality, there are very detailed descriptions, reproduction alerts, collecting hints, and historical backgrounds that will make you an expert in this popular collectible area.

Softcover • 8-1/4 x 10-7/8 • 224 pages
450 b&w photos • 40 color photos
**WDOLL • $22.95**

## The World of Dolls

*A Collectors' Identification and Value Guide*

by Maryanne Dolan

This book is an invaluable reference and price guide. It includes secondary market prices for more than 1,000 dolls and doll-related items and covers doll artists; foreign dolls; doll accessories; paper dolls; and personality dolls from the 1920s to today.

Softcover • 8-1/2 x 11 • 368 pages
300 b&w photos • 28 color photos
**CHADO • $24.95**

## Claire Shaeffer's Fabric Sewing Guide

by Claire Shaeffer

Learn the secrets of selection, wear, care and sewing of all fabrics, including microfibers, stabilizers and interfacings. Content and distinctive properties of each textile are detailed, as are appropriate designs and patterns. Plan and lay out a garment and learn where to obtain equipment and supplies. A wealth of knowledge!

Softcover • 8-1/4 x 10-7/8 • 544 pages
24-page color section
**FSG • $32.95**